SCULPTED:

POETRY

of the

NORTH WEST

SCULPTED:

POETRY
of the
NORTH WEST

Edited by Lindsey Holland and Angela Topping
with an introduction by David Morley

PUBLISHED BY NORTH WEST POETS
Aughton, Lancashire, United Kingdom

Selection by Lindsey Holland and Angela Topping
© Lindsey Holland & Angela Topping

Introduction by David Morley
© David Morley

Individual contributions © the contributors

Submissions reading and editorial advice was provided by
the North West Poets' Board of Editors:
Sheila Hamilton, Lindsey Holland, Sarah Hymas,
Melissa Lee-Houghton, Alec Newman, Angela Topping
and Steven Waling.

First published 2013

Printed and bound in the UK by Biddles, part of the MPG
Printgroup, Bodmin and King's Lynn.

Typesetting by Lindsey Holland

Cover design by The Cover Factory

ISBN   978-0-9575393-0-3   Paperback

CONTENTS

Introduction by David Morley   ix

Martin Figura: Ahem   1
Chris Emery: Bronze   3
Richard Barratt: Post-Box I Love You!   5
Adrian Slatcher: Borges in Beswick   6
Cath Nichols: Tony&Guy   8
V. A. Sola Smith: Downside Up   10
Sarah James: Back on Campus   12
Matt Fallaize: Burscough Street, Ormskirk, 2012   13
Anthony Arnott: From the Window Ledge   14
Richard Barrett: City Council Song   15
Andrew McMillan: from ... protest of the physical   16

Sarah Corbett: To Scale   21
Angela Topping: The Visited   23
Alicia Stubbersfield: Jack   24
Keith Lander: Visiting Mum in Beeston View   25
Pauline Rowe: Sanatorium   26
Janet Rogerson: Confessional   27
Melissa Lee-Houghton: Bringing You Home   28
John Calvert: Running in the Family   30
David Morley: Clearing a Name   31

Geraldine Green: Turning Turtle   37
Jacob Silkstone: Rays at Sea Life Blackpool   39
Clare Kirwan: New Brighton   41
V. A. Sola Smith: Poor Fish   43
Steven Waling: Blackpool Mesostics   44
Sian S Rathore: on fleetwood beach   46
Michael Symmons Roberts: The Drifter And His White
                                         Shadow   48
Liz Loxley: Two Hands   52
Adrian Slatcher: Morecambe Bay   53
JT Welsch: Formby   54

Lindsey Holland: I am Fisherman 59
Elaine Booth-Leigh: This Borrowed Darkness 61
Gill McEvoy: Blakemere: Cheshire 62
Sheila Hamilton: Pete Marsh 63
Lindsey Holland: The Standing 64
Andrew Oldham: Stratum 65

Deryn Rees-Jones: Trilobite 69
Sarah James: Composition 71
David J. Costello: Thor's Rock 72
Andrew Rudd: Jacob's Ladder 73
Gill McEvoy: Beeston Castle, Peckforton Hills 74
Charlotte Henson: Fossil 75
Sarah James: Museum Offering 76
Scott Thurston: Dawn Redwood 77
Scott Thurston: Upperbrook Waterfall 80
Scott Thurston: Otterspool Promenade 83

Eleanor Rees: Saltwater 89
Steven Waling: Leander Swims the Mersey 91
Michael Egan: there by a jarg river he let go a jarg flim 93
Clare Kirwan: Over the Water 95
Pauline Rowe: Goddess, Waiting 96
David Seddon: Sough 98
Andrew Forster: Grange-over-Sands 100

Evan Jones: Cavafy in Liverpool 105
David Seddon: Liver Birds 106
Robert Sheppard: In Unadopted Space 107
Dave Ward: from Where the World Begins 112
Janine Pinion: Department Store, 1965 115
Lindsey Holland: The Port of Liverpool Building 116
Sheila Hamilton: Frequenting the Stanley Palace 117
Pauline Rowe: A Hospital Remembers 118

Steve Waling: Three Cafes in North-East Lancashire 121
Cath Nichols: Miss Lydia Rawlinson takes her tea
with sugar 124

Jan Dean: Deep Cutting   126
Dinesh Allirajah: The Imperfection of Language   127
John Lindley: Ellesmere Port   129
Joy Winkler: Raggedy School   130
John Calvert: The Waters are Freed   131
Emma McCourty: A View from the Top   132
Edwin Stockdale: Mardale   133
Edwin Stockdale: Ravenglass & Eskdale Railway   134
Steph Pike: Forged   135

Daniele Pantano: Vaudeville   139
Andrew Oldham: Two Thousand Year Stare   140
Alison Chisholm: On the Brink   141
V.A. Sola Smith: Punchline   142
Andrew Taylor: November 4th 1978   143
David Tait: Self-Portrait with Terraced Houses   144
Alicia Stubbersfield: In Need of Some Updating   145
Jan Dean: 28 Hanover Street   146
Angela Topping: The Comfort of Hiding   147
Andrew McMillan: not quite   148

Andrew Taylor: The Source that the Brain Prefers   151
Angela Topping: When I was in Widnes and Widnes was
                                    in Lancashire   152
Stephen Beattie: Southport General 5am   153
Martin Figura: Norwich to Liverpool   154
JT Welsch: Ex-Pat on a Northern Train   155
Kim Moore: Train Journey, Barrow to Sheffield   156
Andrew McMillan: neither here nor there   158
Jan Dean: Escape Sequence   160
Andrew Rudd: Journey   161

Janet Rogerson: Forever Unfamiliar   165
John Siddique: I Think of You   166
Kim Moore: Being Married   167
David Riley: Walking to Southport   168
Andrew Oldham: The Last Time We Met   169
Rosie Garland: Walking to Castlerigg   170

Jonny Rodgers: A Piece of a Future   173
Martin Figura: Border   174
Matt Fallaize: Arguably a Horizon   175
Melissa Lee-Houghton: Clowbridge   176
Rachel McGladdery: Amounderness   177

Biographies   181

Acknowledgements   197

INTRODUCTION

By David Morley

On John Speed's 1610 map of Lancashire, the promontory of Amounderness has the Rivers Wyre and Ribble as her north and south and the Forest of Bowland and the Irish Sea as her east and west. As a child I would cycle and pace this ancient Hundred of my county and push my expeditions into the other Hundreds — Lonsdale, Leyland, Salford, Blackburn and West Derby (my folks on my father's side being from Liverpool). I felt I was uncovering constellated worlds, the geology of which was cut and shaped by distinctive climates; and whose borders metamorphosed and became embodied in the accents of people: the six tribes of Lancashire.

Those worlds presented a geography of experience you could cover using your own physical power. Lancashire expanded the imagination by being so intimately all her accents, all her rain, all her Cloughs and fell-sides. I was territorial about every field, hedgerow and town. I felt a competitive distaste for rival counties. What I understood as 'the North West' swelled into a psychological realisation of a greater, wilder, historical Lancashire. As my imagination grew so my idea of the North West of England evolved and deepened, and my perception of it shifted outside of time.

I had been taught how, long after the Battle of Bosworth Field, Lancastrians still wandered the world rehearsing their red rose claims through stories and self-mythologies. How, over the centuries, in Wigan, Bolton and Colne, smoke-stacked sprawls followed and borrowed the verve of the region's rivers. How terraces snuck vertically up the valley-sides, their inhabitants roosting in rows like sparrows. How those who worked and lived in these places created their own spoken poetry, shouted silently between the looms of the mills. And when I cycled through these places as a child, although the mills were hollow and the rivers ran clean of dye, the buildings and streams seemed to bustle with speech and possibility.

It was the possibility of place and language, of reinvention after annihilation: of how place, through its people, could spill sidelong around the world and keep recreating itself in fresh Hundreds. I was nostalgic for both possibility and presence. For my family, Liverpool had offered the exit and entrance for adventure and venture — for Ireland and the New World. When I was tiny, it was where my half-Irish uncles worked their cranes and where they drank. One of my first memories is of being in a pub in Kirkby and falling to sleep atop one uncle's broad, steady shoulders as he wove home late with his pals from the docks. For reasons that would seem naïve today, I went to America for a considerable time, alone at the age of eleven. I took Lancashire with me in my heart and mouth.

As I grew older I came to the understanding that the North West was always larger than Lancashire — before the boundary changes of 1974 exiled Liverpool and Manchester. We looked across to London; we did not look up to it. We disliked those newly imposed borders, yet we could snub the fragmentation because we knew who we were. We had our own special oomph that we occasionally loaned out to the political centre, down south. There was potential energy to our region that the Romanies called Chohawniskey-Tem — 'the White Witches' County'. It was recusant, bolshie and feisty.

Imagined territory possesses, and is never possessed by, any border. The witchy magic of our region did not suddenly cease at The Mersey Tunnel or The Three Shires Stone on the Wrynose Pass. It spilled over — it marauded — across Cheshire's planted plains and into the hills and along the coast roads of North Wales, Westmoreland and Cumberland. The North West is and was always in cultural motion, promotion and commotion — just like its great rival Ridings to the east. The dynamic of reinvention through imagination — of social, cultural and technological restlessness — presents itself every year in the regeneration of the great cities of Liverpool and Manchester. The fact these cities are competitors is part of their charming, uneasy, compatible strength. For underneath them, outside time, lies imagined Lancashire.

The white rose border with the West Riding seemed to be a world apart with its sacrifice stone on the moor: that was where Yorkshire began. On the heights of Lad Law, on those ancient stones incised with Celtic impressions of elk and bison, I would stare back one day and suffer the terms of exile. And what did I see? The fells and valleys of Pendle, Longridge and Bowland shaped by glacier, river and wind. The cup and ring marks carved on that field of life and death. The North West cuts into you. It is what the Welsh call Hiraeth. It is what we might call the feeling of being sculpted. Poetry is one of our vehicles for translating that unspoken emotion from silence.

§

The poems in this marvellous anthology are sculpted and shaped by the experience of living in the North West, with all its real and imagined territories and borders. Many of the home-grown poets in this book take the region as stimulus and subject, deriving clout, gumption and nous from a local habitation and a name. Other poets have settled in the region, bearing with them not only their welcome talents but also artistic panache and a sense for cultural solidarity, a European sense that poetry is an act of community. Universities in the cities and towns teach creative writing. The courses are delivered by some of the best poets in the United Kingdom. In my experience, when an academy is truly part of a community and the community becomes one of the hearts of the academy, the poets are usually the good citizens who have created the symbiosis. That is certainly the case in this region.

The editors Lindsey Holland and Angela Topping set themselves a vigorous task in gathering and sorting the voices of this anthology. Their organisation of the poems into seven movements based around subject and tone is ingenious and generous, as if to the six Hundreds of the old county had been added an imagined Hundred. In essence, the reader has seven shorter books, each of which proceeds from the other, but with the eloquence of space and a deftly selected quotation to set the mood of a poem's moment. I admire how the organisation of this book matches soaring imagination to Lancastrian sagacity. There is no nonsense. There is serious play. There is imaginative geography.

What I felt in particular as I read this anthology was a sense of strong purpose and pleasure — of something artistically fresh and adventurous. I was impressed and delighted that the region I hold most dear to my heart is the home to a standing army of really fine poets whose work is exciting, dynamic and achieved. *Sculpted* is a realisation of a greater North West whose borders are expanding through the many imaginations and voices in this book. I loved it.

David Morley, Warwick, January 2013

SCULPTED:

POETRY

of the

NORTH WEST

'I like to think that the ringroads and parkways echo back further'

Martin Figura

AHEM
After Ginsberg

I saw the best suits of my parents' generation
    destroyed by poor tailoring, synthetic fibres
    and hysterical lapels,
dragging their shopping down the high streets
    of Albion in pacamacs with hairdos under
    hairnets and headscarves,
Brylcream-headed husbands burning pipe tobacco
    in walnut bowls and inhaling through
    the clenched teeth of repressed ardour,
who feared the wind rush in the negro streets
    of Victoriana blowing the sounds and smells
    that threaten the unfamiliar and didn't
    even know Elvis Presley existed yet,
who got drunk on home-made egg-flip at Christmas
    and sang the old songs around the piano
    while their kids were happy with a tangerine
    and dinky toy,
who saved so that one day they might have
    a little car and be saluted by the AA man
    as they drove by,
who were all the time boiling vegetables to eat with
    Spam while listening to the radiogram valves
    singing hot with Family Favourites and after sprouts
    there was Much Binding in The Marsh until
    Billy Cotton cried out WAKEY WAKEY and
    Bandstand glowed out in the deathly grey
    of cathode rays,
who on Fridays went dancing up the club in sixpence
    a week Montague Burton suits and crammed into
    eighteen hour girdles and mail order dresses with
    their blue hair piled on top, but just too soon to have
    been teenagers,

who tripped out to Skegness Vimto-fuelled in charabancs
　　to shine under Billy Butlin's neon "our true intent is all
　　for your delight" while being served brown ale by lasses
　　from Doncaster in grass skirts under plastic palm trees
　　in The Beachcomber Bar,
who never used the front room but kept it pure and the
　　antimacassars pressed for visits by doctors or
　　vicars or teachers for tinned salmon and tinned pears
　　and tinned milk and polished their front steps
　　and never ran out of string,
who knew their place and never thought the universities
　　were for the likes of them but prayed for office jobs
　　for their children and stood for God Save The Queen
　　at The Empire and said how wonderful their policemen
　　were and fought in the war for the likes of me,
who had more words for toilet than the Inuit have for snow
　　and put their teeth in jars then slept in their vests
　　under candlewick counterpanes in cold bedrooms
　　with dreams of winning the pools and bungalows
　　in Cheshire with inside loos and labour saving devices,
who at dawn trod into brown slippers onto cold brown
　　linoleum and could only face the day through the
　　sweet brown haze of a hundred cups of tea and
　　twenty Capstan Full Strength.

BRONZE

You can reach him from the high brick towns
selling fifth-hand carpets or that religion
of furniture near prayer-hoarded townhouses
the trams don't reach. It's a pig sty

beneath those tower blocks
no one remembers being built, then on
through clichés of terracing
under clockwork horizons

accelerating in towards the pointy buildings
at the centre. It's all modern there.
Yet his legacy is clearly housed in all those 60s
movies of The North: the awful accents

almost modish then, where
a backdrop foams with river filth
and the busy wives are shawled with
several kinds of misery and he's

stamping his shoes on bare boards.
It's almost always him the film
revolves on: a bad suit, a bit of rough,
who makes eight hours of crappy stuff

inside a shadowless factory, then we cut
to piled hairstyles dying through
a montage of cavernous dance halls,
not needed. Dipping down by bingo halls

you're in the city now, and take a sudden right
then nestle in beside the crippled stacks
with sundial waste around them:
car parks pricing local absences

for the very few who work here. And arriving
at the nether edge, near the prison or
station or that rectilinear warehouse
partially lettered over gravel bins, you turn

towards a wharf and its rendered dark
of corbels and buttresses showing that sudden
claggy soot no one's cleaned for years,
and slipping into neutral, settle in

to this older dismal district the shoppers
avoid or race through in the city rain.
If you turn your head from all the dirty bits
and walk along the unfenced

artery of the canal, the dead divide
beneath you in their penultimate academies,
nothing but the sewers dream on,
the rivers are sewn back underground

and black clouds from black towns send
their wet truths over all these new accents
of our separate histories.
There are no victories of common purpose.

And turning left, he's there, the one I meant,
a general figure no one reads or recognises
in his bronze assumption, laughable above
some flyposters. I guess he made it here.

Richard Barrett

POST-BOX I LOVE YOU!

Oh post-box
Icon of earlier years
And, more generally
Manchester
I come to celebrate you
Your longevity
And fortitude
And redness
You'll see off all of us
I would never bomb you
Oh post-box, or even
Run a tractor into you
Sentinel, of the Arndale
And Marks and Spencer
Snail-Mail's day
May well have gone
But you

You will live forever

BORGES IN BESWICK

The streets of the Northern Quarter
were my labyrinth years before I knew their names —
late bars recalled only in drunken memory;
many a night mislaid in a Manchester basement.

Did I ever have the native's swagger?
Cutting through to the Apollo wearing Firetrap and
                                        Converse:
rubbing shoulders with the city's familiar faces,
watching New Order play Joy Division songs for the first
                                        time.

Hailing a taxi on a rainy night after a suburban reading,
I wonder how Borges felt, sat beside his mother,
driving round Ardwick, Beswick, Chorlton-upon-Medlock,
looking for Thomas De Quincey's house.

I imagine him holed up in a grubby B&B,
watching Pat Phoenix and William Roache
and leaving us with some knotty puzzle
buried in the foundations of the Arndale.

*

Peering through the clotted air that throttles Manchester,
I realise I've been here longer than anywhere
but haven't made it a home.
The city invites in strangers then keeps its distance.

I like to think that the ringroads and parkways
echo back further, long before the mills and canals,
and that my ancestor, passing by on the turnpike
laid down a marker I have somehow divined.

6

For I travelled north in search of the mist and rain
with scribbled stories and a case full of vinyl,
found poetry in dive bars with sticky floors and sweating
walls
catching glimpses of the future in the ruins of the past.

Could I reverse the journey and step out in the Buenos
Aries night
would I be any closer to life's elemental puzzles?
Just as Borges did, searching for a glimpse of another's gold
Stashed in the shadows where he once walked.

Cath Nichols

TONI&GUY
Canal Street, Manchester

The Union

Queers existed in the red light district, in a few minging basement bars let out on weekday nights. It is 1978, Manchester. You are eighteen and a man asks you to be a hair model, he likes your sharp male features. Vidal Sassoon is something new, the hub of something hot. Gay men fancy you, straight women fancy you and certain lesbians do too. You play bass in a band, support Joy Division; you are The Distractions.

Paradise

Your band gets signed to Factory Records up on Paradise Street. Your band then moves to Island. The old office becomes a club, the Paradise Factory. I meet friends at Manto's then queue for Paradise. Manto is Canal Street's first gay bar with floor-to-ceiling windows, a revolution in visibility. We display our Flesh at the Hacienda, drink water. Wave our hands in the air. We do, we do care.

Poptastic

'We're here, we're queer, and we're not going shopping!' we chant at Pride. Except of course we are, overcome with amazement that we carry a pink pound. City living rocks, except factory lofts are becoming dear. A glossy mag for gay gals has arrived: *Diva*. With its personal ads and photos, we're so excited pre-web. When we tire of Paradise, its techno-beat and dykes in wonderbras, we go to Poptastic, dance in lace-up boots. A term for under-aged flirts: the baby-dyke.

Velvet

When I'm twenty-eight a man in a nightclub touches my hair, so he touches me. No-one touches a No.1 without stroking the fuzzy-felt scalp of it. And this is post-rave, post-E, when we all drink beer, so the guy that fondles my head is a little too forward, a little too straight. But, turns out he's a straight *hairdresser* who wants to hand-cut my skin-head. He works at Toni&Guy, gives me his card.

Cruz 101

I wonder if a cut will feel different to a shave? I go to the salon, let him snip-snip away, but it feels the same. Someone bleaches my hair —I look ill. I'm asked to walk the walk at the hair show flexing a riding crop. Without the example of David Beckham, his thousand quid blond skinhead, I don't think this cut could've happened. Bless. David Beckham made me a hair model.

Spirit

Do you remember Anna? When Big Brother was an unknown quantity? We all had a crush on her. Same year you and I started dating. Anna had been a nun, played guitar and sang. It emerged she had a girlfriend. Maybe Anna had a shaved head as a novice nun. She has a bob now and is more than the sum of her parts to us. It's the year 2000. The year I let my hair grow out, the year I grow it long.

V.A. Sola Smith

DOWNSIDE UP

There must be millions like us
lost or tossed off this way,
penny by penny,

like they are worthless. Here
the Metrolink collects them up,
folding down its Fagin palm seats.

Emptying out the pockets
of greater Manchester,
we ride the Pied Piper

from Ladywell to Mediacityuk.
My sire taught me of the goldmine route.
Behind the back of Piccadilly

the Tib Street Horn and Afflecks Palace
rub shoulders like pimps, on their watch
for latchkey babies who lose their way.

But, of all those who sold their day
to come out and play, here I am.
I dipped into the night like ink

and I wrote a letter to you
on the flipside of the old Coliseum,
waiting a dealer's length.

For the brief passing of your white ship
kids press themselves like graffiti
or blood against the alley walls, or more

like rows and rows of abandoned poems
filling the back pages of an exercise book,
to become nothing more than screwed up.

BACK ON CAMPUS

Noise wakes me just after 1am. Barely
a scraping of snow on the pavement
and three students are attempting
to sculpt themselves a small man.
Their laughter sends flakes flying. It layers
the street and rolls into six feet drifts
that block the road, cover cars, choke
cold doorways. I watch through a window
which won't open, wipe the mist
of my breath. Above the roofs' jagged edges,
two cranes hold up the sky's tarpaulin.
Stars glint through holes. I feel the temptations
of height — that fear of falling, not flying,
held distant by glass. I always take the stairs,
step by concrete step, four floors up
to this cubicled room's disturbed-sleep view.
And now the snow has stopped,
the students have gone, laughter is turned
to slush. As I leave my breath's mist
to cool, I think of places I've been:
cities of cranes, strangers, snow,
and here, night-lit city of all these
brick-edged, broken heights.

BURSCOUGH STREET, ORMSKIRK, 2012

Offer leaflets drifting
on carved stone

been a banner
year for
makers of
clearance sale
banners

Anthony Arnott

FROM THE WINDOW LEDGE

These streams,

interlocking bubbles of festivity.

The rozzers   do nothing
if people   do nothing
wrong. Weed, face paint, revelry.

All the lights are green on Victoria Street,
birds-eye view of birds.

Crowds and queues, fathers for justice
                                    jump
until the rozzers have nothing to do
                                        except
                                            tell

                        us
                                                    to
                                        climb
                            back
                                    inside.

Richard Barrett

CITY COUNCIL SONG

Gone, Cannon Street
Become, 'new' Cannon Street
With a roof on it
Unrecognisable, now
The Cannon Street
Of my youth

No more, Cromford Court
No more, multi-storey
No more, huge bus-station even
    (sigh)
Or through access
    to Piccadilly
Just a branch of Next
Where I applied for a job once
Which I failed to get

Manchester, I awoke one morn(ing)
To find the map redrawn
And my favourite street gone

You're always changing, Manchester, yet
You're always the same

Andrew McMillan

FROM ... PROTEST OF THE PHYSICAL

lame arm of the crane   circling
unstocked shelves of half built car park
the day's spent itself already   so early in the evening

 so early in the evening to be spent   to want sleep   to brush
 off our shirts as crumbs the advances of another   too often
 I've said love   tongue to spine   too long spent not touching

a man   alone
a room with a hundred TV screens
                                talk

                                 town as talk
           town as a dialogueheavy scene from a Ken Loach film
                    town as a hundred TV screens

the barrelswagger of a man
benched in bandstands with empty
vials of people sitting

                       sleepdeprived and shaking
                       redfaced   drinking
             or already drunk and drinking

*

days pivot in their sockets so quickly
station   a girl's sudden
flurry of fists   unroosting of doves

around a young labourer's head   and all journey his face
is somewhere between a carving and a glass of moving
water
and his face is covered in paint   its tear stained

*

field   way home
neighbour with her dog   a man flying
a model aircraft   just like a real plane   only smaller

'… If you stay dead I will read you poems.
I will walk for miles with prayers in my heart like
coronary balloons'

Sarah Corbett

TO SCALE

My grandfather, armchair socialist, trade unionist, bus
                                                    driver,
one hand pale in summer, shining with grafted skin
from just caught, thrown back fire of a grenade in the war,
was a weekend hobbyist of World's Fair scale replicas:
                                                    traction

engines, fairground organs, and then, The Gallopers,
a carousel revolving amidst the first years of my childhood
little scenes like a magic lantern, a making of wonders
I was witness to but never allowed to touch, not the gold

in the grooves of manes or tiny tough seeds of hooves,
not the out flung tails that were like delicate flames
and could be snipped out easy as a candle's, or across loins
and curled about necks like girdles, painted names

of horses never quite *perfect,* never quite *finished,*
always one or other technical hitch in the mechanism
that made each ride its pole as the platform turned,
or glitch in the musical box that churned out the tune

I'd associate with a pair of miniature Dutch clogs
in the glass cabinet which also housed a Victorian
china headed doll in a black dress, in mourning,
and a family of crystal swans in glassy suspension;

my grandfather, good with eye and hand, and why not,
                                                    artist,
some-time jobbing engineer for Billy Smart, descendent
of attendants to the court of Richard, Lords of the Marches
at the behest of William for services at the conquest of
                                                    England,

21

who turned down the travelling circus and moved one
county
his whole life, a sideways step like a waltz from Shropshire
to Cheshire;
who'd quote, not just those blue remembered hills, but
the land of lost content, I see it shining, who made a studio

of the middle room to work his unattended dreams to scale.

Angela Topping

THE VISITED

How mum came to know them I never knew;
their only friend, she took them food parcels,
ran errands, offered chatter like coins,
and sometimes clothes. And always, she took me,
as though a child's face could give them hope.

At mum's knock, they'd open doors a scared
two inches, then wider. Straight in from the street
to rooms stuffed with knick-knacks:
wax blooms and stuffed birds under a dusty dome;
bronze stags; crinoline girls, and cranberry glass.

Remnants of servants from big houses,
not encouraged to marry, they retired
to nurse decaying parents in rented terraces,
then folded sheets over their dead faces.

Behind yellowed lace, they slept downstairs,
bedrooms an Everest away and bitter cold.
easier not to have to use the chamber pot,
nothing to go upstairs for, anyway.

Everything about them scared me:
The staleness of their breath, their skin
engraved with dirt, and most of all
the thought of one day being them.

Alicia Stubbersfield

JACK

A gambler, winning the house and land at poker,
coming home in someone else's Mercedes
after a night playing cards, doing a deal.
At shows your daughters hid their horses
so you couldn't be reminded, use them as collateral.

You were calm enough to make men parachute out
of planes, to clear Auschwitz after the war. I dived
under water, picked up a brick when you trained
the pentathlon team. *It's only money* you said,
now you had plenty after years working in St Helens'
chip shops and the welding factory, still washed
and shaved in the kitchen, embarrassing your wife
who tolerated unmarked saddles in the hall,
boxed crystal cigarette lighters piled up, strange visitors.

The cortege mapped St Helens' narrow streets.
We drank your favourite *La Flora Blanche,*
told stories about you and laughed.
You'd said life wouldn't be worth living without a deal:
the wad in your back pocket just ready to peel,
notes pressed into a hand before you shook on it.

VISITING MUM IN BEESTON VIEW

The place has a smell of its own, a school, a farm.
Yesterday she thought it was was an airport.
Today I find her dozing in her bedroom,
plonk myself on the plastic covered chair.
       What do YOU want?
Good start.
       Look at that thing, over there.
It's a framed photo, on her dressing table.
Two people, strangers.
       Those are my daughters.
She always wanted daughters.
I change the subject.
Would you like to go out today?
       Yes, I'm fed up with this hotel,
       the waitresses are bitches.
She laughs a laugh that's not her laugh.
       They took them away in buses.
Who? I ask.
       The Poles. They were up to no good.
I'm tempted to say 'not the Welsh then?'
       Your brother built this hotel.
Yes, I know mum, clever isn't he?
I tell her I like her skirt.
       It's nice isn't it? I pinched it.
Doris comes in wearing mum's coat.
       CLEAR OFF YOU.
       They've let a load of Welsh move in you know.
Well, I'm sure they had good reason.
       You don't know anything. Are you my brother?
I don't rise to this, but go and sign her out,
return to find her naked in the corridor.

Pauline Rowe

SANATORIUM

I think of the disease as a person.
He kept me from my home, my childhood, love —
a tall and slender, dark-haired man — I gave
my younger years to him. Streptomycin
sounds so clinically simple. You forget
the endless, silent waiting on Winter days,
the tap-tap of matron's feet, the ways
a child can grieve for the living, can set
himself against the world when illness takes
away the touch of love, the joy of dirt,
the impossible sorrow of years
on the faces of your Mum, Dad, brother;
how, in old age, that sanatorium
ice-cold separation still bites, still hurts.

CONFESSIONAL

I remember my father
his eyes round as a chicken
his jacket of seaweed.

I remember his perfume
of flour and coal
his hair sleek as my father's.

I remember my mother
her eyes knitted blue
her shoes of white marble.

I remember her voice
her unholy recitals
her hair black as my mother's.

I remember my parents
their eyes like two murderers
their love like the hangman.

I remember the priest
eyes flecked with our sins
his robes full of dinner.

I remember my childhood
laughing like injustice
eyes like forgetting.

Melissa Lee-Houghton

BRINGING YOU HOME

I looked at the flat where you died, on a digital photograph.
A four storey whitewashed house with starlings
nesting in the gutters, bay windows and plenty of light.

I imagined you were painting a masterpiece there,
by the seafront and living off Nescafe and fish and chips.
Mum reckoned you'd gone there to convalesce —

Colwyn Bay was like that in the nineties.
I plan to travel to this place that I don't know,
get to know the geography, not just this architecture of
                                                    dreams —

a whitewashed house has receded into my unconscious.
Here the landscape is different but I feel
you could have benefitted from the warmth of strangers

and not just the tobacconists and dealers.
I am bringing you home to me,
carrying you all these miles with my viscera,

flying you in through an open window and putting you
to bed. If you stay dead I will read you poems.
I will walk for miles with prayers in my heart like coronary
                                                    balloons

filling with hot blood. It's heavy, this bereavement
twelve years delayed. I walk with a dual longing
for life and for death. I pace up the council estate on the
                                                    outskirts

to the suburbs where we could never afford to live,
blackbirds squabbling in the brambles.

I walk to the war memorial where we used to go drinking
                                        as kids

because it was lit up at night; the tree where we carved
our names has been felled. Some things here die without a
                                        trace —
I've come so far to find you. Your daughters

didn't attend your funeral. They didn't lay flowers or
                                        grieve.
Tonight I walk to my first boyfriend's red brick house
                                        where
we would smoke roll-ups out of the window on schooldays,

it has been up for sale five times in two years.
His dad bled to death there, his stepdad kept a gun. I
                                        believe
that the sublimated energy of a place can carry on

over miles and miles and into your arms whether you heed
                                        it or not.
The photograph is all I've got but you've become so
                                        indefinable
in my mind that when I sleep I am peeling back bed-sheets,

unlocking cold eyelids and knees; I am stood
at the window staring out at the sea I cannot connect with
in my world of woods where kids make fires and get
                                        wasted

and still waters which are the shadow of death
and open plains which are the shadow of death
and dilapidated buildings which are the shadow of death.

John Calvert

RUNNING IN THE FAMILY

Outside the family, I ran faster
My three uncles lapping the war
Builder, sailor, draughtsman
They stayed on the circuit
Rounded the grey marathon towns
With a parade of urban,
Cheshire aunties
Sprinting in the other direction
Did I shake them off?

David Morley

CLEARING A NAME

Spindrift across Stalmine, a place you won't know.
Reedbeds, Gyp sites; flat Lancashire's Orinoco.

I watch a mistle-thrush on a blown telegraph wire,
leave my car by the dead elm above the river.

The camp is two caravans. The police have just left.
Two blue-tacked Court Orders this wind can't shift

or the rain read. A girl squatting with a carburettor
on her bare knees. Another, older, in a deck-chair

spoons Pot Noodle. Their dad with his pride, no joy,
wrestles over the yawning bonnet of a lorry.

Mam is out, knocking Blackpool's door
with her basket of tack, toddler dressed-down with care

for the rending detail: no shoes. I watch
the father unbend, fumble at the fire, splice a match

from a stray half-wicker, then I come down.
He lets a welcome wait in another time,

twists a roll-up, nods OK to his staring daughters.
Eyes me like fresh scrap fenced from a dealer,

half-sorted, half-known. Yes; he knew our family
"more for what they were" — Hop-girls, Iron-boys —

"but they married out, and there's the end of it.
Your muck's paid no muck of ours a visit".

31

A thin smile: "Except your dad,
he came with the nose of Concorde

on worksheets reeking of grease and swarfega,
bleating 'an inch is now a bloody centimetre'.

What's up with your schools? I'd say. Him — 'This *is* school'.
We squinnied blueprints as if they were braille.

Taught ourselves ground-up. A small conversion.
If your muck had stayed in family, if your gran

not gone nosing *gaujo* like they were the end-all.
Now you've had your end, fair do's. Get off pal,

you're not burnt up on fags or dodgy work."

The ends, we want; the means are half the work:

something in his grip, under my sleeve like veins,
where hands lock together, become the same,

'Arctic on Antarctica' ... *I need background.*
The uncle on my mother's side. "Pulled from a pond.

The police were out for a man. Any Taig or Gyp.
Guns broke for a chicken-shoot. They found him face-up

and it fitted. They shot shite in a barrel."
That B-road where Lancashire discharges its spoil.

Split mattresses. Paint tins. Grim stuff in carriers.
The sign No Dumping No Travellers.

I make my way back to the car, running
the hard keys from hand to hand then, turning,

pocket them. I do not move. It is not smart to show
(that plain car by the woods) how and where you go.

One uncle of mine went swimming. His name is snow, or thaw, or mud. And you wouldn't know.

'…we rode along the promenade as kids,

waiting for the night to tear across the
shore line'

———————————————————————

Geraldine Green

TURNING TURTLE

I startled the lark. Perhaps I was walking
too fast, or the sudden arm movement
as I lifted the ball-on-a-rope for my dog,
disturbed the air, swung the lark up on
its cry as it carried itself skywards, its song
settled from surprise to what sounded like
scolding. That was at the end of my ramble.
I parked the car, strode past the bent by
the wind blown hawthorn, its thin, stunted
branches pointed north and I followed,
folding myself around the contours of
sheep tracks through low growing gorse.
Vicious, if you have to retrieve a ball
from its centre.

Today it was me and the wind,
couples, singles, families, dogs, kites and
the occasional phlegmatic sheep.
I sat on a limestone rock, watched waves
nibble at the shore of Chapel Island, chatted

with a couple and their blonde haired daughter,
afraid of Roy until her father threw the roped ball
and she grew braver. They wandered off,
laughing, towards the stone circle, soon to be
decorated with pumpkins, chrysanths and candles.
The Bay, a dazzle of waves, even at this distance —
I could hear them mumbling to pebbles and marram,
down there on the beach at Bardsea where, as a child,
I once ducked as dad warned the family, 'Bees!'.
And a dense, fast cloak of them swarmed over
our heads as we lay flat on our picnic blanket.

Sometimes we would play in the gulleys,
turned turtle by a sudden slap of wave,
happy among cockles and the smell of salt mud.
I can still feel it dried and grey between my toes,
scraping it off before pulling on plimsolls,
heading home with a bag of shells
and a bunch of memories to give dad
when he came in from work at the Strep. Plant,
Glaxo, smelling of pear drops and acid.

Jacob Silkstone

RAYS AT SEA LIFE BLACKPOOL

Wednesday evening, last week of the Illuminations
and the wind begins to turn the Promenade
into a one-way walk. The queue for Harry Ramsden's
stretches half the Golden Mile. In the early winter dark
I find myself outside the Sea Life Centre. I retreat,
needing enough bars to make a call.
When I get through, he tells me 'a few more weeks'.
I hang up, stand a second in the October cold.

Inside, I'm in time for the last talk on rays.
I watch one press its paleness to the glass,
nosing close to the stunted crowd; its mouth apes
a marathon runner's metronomic gasps.
Their skin is made of placoid scales —
don't put your hands in, but it feels rough
from tail to head, smooth from head to tail.
They're vulnerable, there aren't enough
outside captivity and they mature late,
we know the population's in decline
and if we don't act now, meaning today,
we'll be up against it, we just don't have time …

The talk ends and the rays turn, work their measured loops
of the long cage. Only one remains
at the surface, navigating in small unhurried slaps,
before sinking slowly under, pectoral fins
tapping a valediction on the water, like the open
hand of a drowned man … Perhaps two more weeks

and it's over. I'm still holding the phone,
wrong way up, so tight the plastic creaks
or seems to creak: I'm no longer sure.
The rays butt blindly against the tank, *they feed
by smell*, move like numbed fingers at a locked door,
we just don't have time ... another week ...

Clare Kirwan

NEW BRIGHTON, 1978

So easy to find myself there —
every hill led to the edge of land.
I'd freewheel without thinking
grey brown river. It meant nothing
to me, yet I sought it out —
its brackish solitude and always
the wind — sometimes a howl
you understand, sometimes a sob.

All the wrong way around. I was
too young for such nostalgia
but Seasons in the Sun
stirred up my teething soul.
Those were the days
of blue anorak, battered,
big glasses, briny,
bad hair tattered flags.

The prom was then, as now,
unlovely and all at right angles —
an expanse of pavement, lampposts,
railings, concrete wall, and then
the pirate fingertips of Irish Sea
hypnotizing, enticing me
to that churning horizon.

And going home seemed further
than the journey out had been.
So easy to find myself there,
then turning, realizing the wind

had been behind and pushing.
Head down, salted, gripping handlebars,
fighting back weather and inclination,
thirteen and against everything.

V.A. Sola Smith

POOR FISH

Shell suits, crushed by the sagging tarpaulin of Asian fabric
stalls, in penny arcades, and sneaking to redemption
games beyond the crack exterior of shooting galleries
and the crack reality of shooting galleries, a whisper

between the isles of bargain basement food stuff stores,
stealing from the ginnells and cobbled snickets, the not-yet
ghouls, tripping unseen about their fate like the helter
                                    skelter
fun house stairs, we rode along the promenade as kids,

waiting for the night to tear across the shore line, faceless
and fearless and one against the jetstream of the whole
                                    North
Atlantic, bellowing then at each raised hand till it shattered
at our feet, powerless to salt even our sneaker soles,

launching kisses and slaps in the dark, desperate
to pull and push and plummet deeper
and farther into the prize draw rock pools
the sea spits all the poor fish into like shells.

We were just kids, trying our luck against the killer tide,
downing fluorescent alcohol and sparking rough cut green,
careless, rogues seeds whizzing and bursting,
every night, vandalising the ocean's ssh approach
like fireworks, raging to break through the bore.

Steven Waling

BLACKPOOL MESOSTICS

where The gulls are
skriking over auntIe's guest house
on long boreD days
spending porriDge-lukewarm mornings
in tobacco waLlpapered
amusemEnt arcades
do trY to be happy

oh I dO like to be
soMewhere other than here

end of the Pier blue jokes
let's go On with the show
dad's mild Mum's babycham

by the Penny-slot sea
even then alOne boy
not hoMe anywhere

I do like To be beside
the fIsh'n'chip waves
the lemonaDe front
the canDyfloss beach
the scrapping guLls in beery air
the sEa's breaking over
the skY's blue valance

the clOuds' teastain
the rain proMenade

44

breathing the Pleasure Beach
atmOsphere playing
naughty postcard Music

dipPing toes
in the wish yOu were here
wet dreaM ocean

beside the Teenage golden
swimsuIt surf where
girls lifteD skirts for
boys their sanDcastle hopes
and my sLim chances
the sExy young
I hardlY understand

am I a ghOst on your
caMera

under the Pier grappling
with the sea cOming in over
condoM waves

so hapPy they dance
kiss me slOwly boys
buMper car girls

Sian S. Rathore

ON FLEETWOOD BEACH

in these shingled beaches, summer laps in,
cool sand beige
the grey sea licks against it summons up
the kiss of what I could not then predict
that I would miss

the rock-pools round the seaweed glint
and shock my mother's eyes so she retreats
into a husband's grasp who defends her sight
with an arm

i sit. apparently my hair is like liza minelli's. i
am six or seven and no frills pop is popping with
joy on my tongue like caviar, as he tries to carve
a watermelon with a swiss-army knife
which reminds mum of her dad.

easterly, when sun slows down, a Prussian blue
for moments, dances through fleetwood's skies
like northern lights. remembering, I could not
know this model's grasp could actually let

go, and now sun sleeps, or rests, our
shadows say it's time for home, and ghosts of
gulls and lemonade and castles long kicked down

circle my memories. we were so happy driving home,
the tussles in the car regarding who would sing which
part and yet now — I see my mother rooted in loss.
fifteen years ahead — the beach a melting sugarscape

glittering shingles and burning grass, leading to beach
it might bring about a memory, or two, or ten thousand;
my thoughts run with them, now

the unforgiving night comes in. the view from our
front room, the farmers lighting fires, the
cows marauding up and down then sleep — they
settle — it will rain quite soon

and we exhale a memory. we are resigned. there
are no lights for him (but once a year they shine
like birthday balloons, with auras), just the sediments
of recall. the arguments at morning, the

making up by noon, the squabbling at dinner
then the giggling at supper — though we do not
have him, we still have
the sun, the summer, the beach towels —

and doughnuts still sprinkled with sugar and sand.

Michael Symmons Roberts

THE DRIFTER AND HIS WHITE SHADOW

I

Yes, the white shadow.
Sounds like a super-hero,
looks like an absence,
smells brackish, of mussel husks.
I struggle for more detail.

II

I sleep on the beach,
at the cutting-edge where blades
of star and ocean
whet against a belt of sand.
Night by night it sharpens me.

III

No matter how dark
my coat, how wide-brimmed my hat,
I print a blank shape.
My heels bruise the salt-drenched shore,
but sun gapes steely though me.

IV

White is not absence,
but an over-abundance,
colours on colours.
A shadow is not semblance,
more source, more maker's study.

V

Is it my own death,
stalking me, obsessed with me,
rehearsing the chalk
outline of my corpse? If so,
I do admire its patience.

VI

Is it a shadow
on an x-ray, elvers in
the alveoli,
swimming upstream to my mouth,
coughing out my final words?

VII

Or is it my form,
see-through, gentle, soul on strand,
at home in its skin?
It plays like a child, safe, sound,
I could watch it all day long.

VIII

I live on seafood.
My shadow lives on thin air.
No hound of heaven
chasing me down days and nights,
just a stray cur at my heels.

IX

We are related,
flesh-ghost. There is a purpose
in your hounding me.

Maybe one day I'll turn tail
and follow you, in silence.

X

I try to drown you,
drag you out into the waves,
but you come clearer,
even as your face is slit
by coral, as your throat floods.

XI

Genes of sand, these grains
are rummaged by the backwash.
They could turn ocean,
or may chance upon the codes
for ice-fields, mountains, forests.

XII

My shadow's gene-map
is identical to mine.
We are siamese,
joined at the feet, each of us
dependent on our soles' welt.

XIII

Summer, and shadows
sardine the beaches. My scared
albino brother
disappears all afternoon.
We meet again at low tide.

XIV

Walking the tide-line,
You try to link arms, hold hands.

Foam clings to driftwood,
bottles (no messages), weed.
Back off. I barely know you.

Liz Loxley

TWO HANDS

They work in tandem
  wind and water
      chipping at limestone
  shaping the sand;
today,   the shore
is etched with worry
    grooved
with frown lines;
   they have cast
     stones,
      pebbles that rest
  in your palm
  like the heart
  of a gull;
 you can hear them
singing as they work.

Adrian Slatcher

MORECAMBE BAY

Light mithers
Through grey clouds

Solitary figures
Pick their way across the bay

Tread on
The soft sands

Light reflects
Off the walls of the Midland Hotel

Returning
But not knowing what I'll find

I plagiarise
Memory again

Under the duvet
Reading Henry Fielding

The smell of you retained
In the folds of my shirt.

FORMBY

Individual mudflats and sandflats, embryonic
shifting dunes. Fixed and mobile dunes
of the mobile dune system by humid dune slacks
upon dune grasslands. Dune heat among the reedbeds
beds various other bedforms at Formby, ringed
with ringed plover, grey plover, grey-haired
grey hair grass and bar-tailed godwit. Knot, dunlin,
stable bar features on the foreshore, near the windfarm.
Liverwort, penny and sneeze wort, sea sandwort.

Sand sedge, sea spurge, wood sage, sand couch, sea kale,
sea rocket, sand lizard, sandwinning, sanderling.
Sea holly, see sandhill rustic moth, and most mosses,
saltmarsh, polypody, kidney vetch, then restharrow.
Wintering waterfowl, individual waders on the strandline.
Helleborine. Carline thistle, horsetail, cat's tails or
cat's ears, mouse-eared hawkweed, hawksbeard, colt's foot,
bird's foot trefoil, viper's bugloss, false catgrass, true bee
orchid, marsh orchid, or $10,000 pyramidal orchid.

Do dewberry. Catch oystercatcher and scattered bricks,
or broken brick chimneys for sea defences, and famed
natterjack toads, known locally as the Bootle Organ.
Dogs, still and silent in their station wagon pens.
The world's first world's first lifeboat station.
Two dads with two girls. Two mums with two girls'
four wellies. The fantastic great-crested newt, yellow-
horned poppy, or too few few-flowered spike-rush.
Shy red squirrels acquiescing to American grays.

The red deer's 5000-year-old footprints on or in
the beach, with those of the auroch, the last of which
died in Poland, 1627, before the initial resilience
of the Saxons when the Vikings rowed from Ireland,

before the last launch from the lifeboat station was
filmed, 1916, before the Romans, before the railway
bringing human manure from Liverpool, before
Liverpool, well before your uncle, the chemist,
was born and eventually reborn Father Formby.

'In time we cut a swathe through ourselves, through woods, fields, across waters —'

Lindsey Holland

I AM FISHERMAN

I walk your stepping stone hills, circle lakes,
stride over bogland, moor, canal, venture
through towns where mills offer crumbled chimneys
to sleeping nests. I'm shadow quick.

My hands are the size of terraces, barnacle rough,
reddened by western gales. I knot them through
the nylon of my trawl net. It follows me

down cobbled slopes where my feet
break cracks into potholes; it gathers brown bottles
and green bins, sandwich boards, nightclub flyers.

On thundering nights, I prefer the coast, begin
at the lip of Grange-over-Sands, head south.
As quicksand kisses my boots, I listen
for the cockles' clack working razor clams to powder

and wade toward Heysham where the net
pulls artefacts from mud below hollows
that bodies once filled. I stoop until my nose
collects a hint of genome.

Your cities lure me in autumn. I pass
by shifting trees where pigeons hide their faces,
read adverts for networks, pause at hotel windows
where couples lie sweated, drunk, and executives bend
over Spotified laptops and cold instant coffee.

I thread my net through buses at the depot,
drag thumb-greased tickets, abandoned gloves, boxes
of ready-made chicken bones spotted with lipstick.

Later, I curl in the arch below the railway line
and count my haul, imagine how every item altered you.

Elaine Booth-Leigh

THIS BORROWED DARKNESS

When we arrived at the shore it chilled us —
there's a darkness here we fought with flames.

Through generations' mixing of genes,
we roll back the night, take hold of language,
re-build structures, absorb our rites.

In time we cut a swathe through ourselves,
through woods, fields, across waters —
our names go down like nine-pins in the long telling.

Trading in a rainbow of skins
we find tin, wool and sugar at tea-times
under grey clouds, and efface ourselves in concrete.

The earth we borrow is bread to others —
they stare, and hold our darkness in their bones.

Gill McEvoy

BLAKEMERE, CHESHIRE

The pines are muttering in tongues;
beyond their wall of blackness lies
a shining lake,

alive and loud with colonies of gulls.
I want to go there,

search for
purple skullcap at the water's edge.

The wind picks up, the trees begin
to crack from side to side like whips,
their mutter turns to roar.

I run the terrifying
gauntlet of the pines,

burst
into a First Created world,

silver with light and water,
glittering with wings.

Sheila Hamilton

PETE MARSH
for the Lindow Man

Pete Marsh they name him.
It's never easy to deal
with a *nameless* man,

to haul a nameless man free
from his home,
drive him to the mortuary.

So, Pete Marsh he is,
though dead a while.

Mr Marsh becomes a major story,
is not long in the mortuary,
is off to London for tests and storage.

Still, in his way,
he's in Lindow Moss, sleepyhead
within the peat. Reeds
nudge him, fogs, damps, tree-stumps,

touching this leather-bag,
this grimace.

Lindsey Holland

THE STANDING

October cold, we stand on the spur
and point to Jodrell Bank. The spur

is slithering wet. Pillars of smoke
rise from the flatland below the spur

where cars might move but the hunters in us
only notice glints, from where the spur

appears like an anvil, grey bulk hunched,
no visible figures. You ask about the spur

and I tell you a glacier: we were cut
from brutal water, bouldered. The spur

survived, at least in part, like the two of us,
healthy, clambered, cracked. The spur

has known the pressure of Celtic leather feet,
accepted spears. Blood sullied the spur's

infinite sediment, layers of Roman,
Saxon and Tudor genome. The spur

absorbs our footprints, rain, the cow shit,
and warrens collapsed, reformed. The spur

will swill and knock us down to an archive.
We scramble home. We stand on the spur.

STRATUM

We find rooms full of boxes; musty, mildew cracking air,
tracks of a boar scraped along the skirting.
Tusk scented, wire brush bristle spine, digging down.
With spade, pick, hammer and shovel comes the past.

Tracks of a boar scraped along the skirting.
The ghost of a tussle in the kitchen, battle bones in the hall.
With spade, pick, hammer and shovel comes the past,
arrow heads, pike and drums still sounding in the lounge.

There are shoes in the wall, iron nails in the wood,
the ghost of a tussle in the kitchen, battle bones in the hall;
arrow heads, pike and drums still sounding in the lounge.
We find carved names in the stone that covered the wild
                                                    men;
bulls that bellow behind stone walls looking to be free.

There are shoes in the wall, iron nails in the wood.
Layers added, covered over, buried behind veneer.
Carved names in the stone that covered the wild men.
Stone walls, black concrete, cover carvings and names.

We hear bulls that bellow behind stone walls looking to be
                                                    free.
The forgotten men, billowing bulls, given up as burnt
                                                    offerings.
Layers are added, covered over, buried behind veneer;
stone walls, black concrete, cover carvings and names.

Tusk scented, wire brush bristle spine, digging down,
the forgotten men, billowing bulls, given up as burnt
                                                    offerings.
We find rooms full of boxes; musty, mildew cracking air.

'This fossil alters the shape of my palm.
Flesh moulds to its mineral hardness'

Deryn Rees-Jones

TRILOBITE

Remember, as a child, how someone would shout *Catch!*
and too old to refuse, and too young not to —
the body's coordinates not quite set

this object, moving in an arc towards you
somehow created you, trembling, outstretched?
That's how it came to me, this trilobite,

a present from the underworld, a stern familiar
hopelessly far-fetched. What it wanted from me
I never knew, its hard parts being its only parts,

the three parts of its crossways nature
cephalos, thorax, pigidium
as later, now, I've learned to call them,

carrying a memory of itself like water
as my fingers moved on its captive body,
the feathery stone of its cool guitar.

It reminded me of a woodlouse, too,
the honesty of small, friendly things.
But the metallic gleam of its smoothed edges

were taut and innocent as an unfired gun.
So it bedded in, leaving behind a gleaming trail
as a biro bleeding in a pocket might,

a puff of ink from a hounded squid.
And my skin shimmered
with its silvery threads, and my breath quickened

as it wrote my body, left a garden of knowing in damp
tattoos.

The further I threw it, the closer it came.
Sometimes, alone, I'd ask it questions

stroke it like a secret pet
How deep is the ocean? What's the blueness of blue?
How is the earth as you lie inside it?

It would reply in a voice both
high-pitched and enduring, or
whisper like a ghost till only silence remained.

And left me only when I'd learned to love it,
small as a bullethole,
in the place where it pressed itself

its fossil colours close to my heart.
Last night, unable to sleep
it nudged its way back into my life,

pulling me from the fragrant pillow
to perch once again on my naked shoulders,
to drop like a coin in my offered hand.

Beside me, my husband slept.
And the fact of its presence, its subtle truth,
was something to touch,

like the wounds of Christ.
Its transformation as I went to kiss it,
a wafer on the pushed out tongue.

Sarah James

COMPOSITION

I lay down on the forest floor to sleep.
Friends made me a pillow of peat, a warm
swamping cover. My leafy bed hardened.
Voices seeped the seams of my deep-coaled dreams.

Kershaw. Lower Yard. King. China. Pasture.

Bang! Shaken awake to dark rock, muffled
shouting, bells, a smell of sulphur and smoke,
I felt myself fall; then jolt, judder, jolt...
a cranking jerk and sudden lurch upwards.

Pasture-china-king-lower yard-kershaw.

The vibrations stopped. A hammer tap, crack,
and my iron bed split. Birdsong and light
rushed in, while our fossilised tale slipped out,
as strangers read the fern seeds in their palm.

David J. Costello

THOR'S ROCK

This is where a God bled
His calcified clot scarred the land
In a pool of petrified ripple

Freighted with runnels of pigment
The red glyphed surface holds history
For those who can read it

Across the River Dee
The Welsh Winter prepares its fist
Each icy knuckle turbulent with iron

The off-cut from some vast amputation
Dusk's filter brushes your skin black
Perfecting your shadow

Note: Thor's Rock is a sandstone outcrop at Thurstaston, Cheshire. It is part of a former Viking settlement.

Andrew Rudd

JACOB'S LADDER

Near the end of the walk
a choice: a long loop
of wooden steps, or this
sandstone clamber.

Only a scramble up the cliff
but it feels like a climb.
It's no contest. These days
I always choose the rock.

A vertical gully,
four niches for your feet.
Two finger-holds
to get you onto the ledge.

Turn, pivot on a root,
look down on treetops.
Zigzag over bolsters
of red sandstone,

each step too high to be easy.
How good it feels to be
back on the top path,
out of breath.

Gill McEvoy

BEESTON CASTLE, PECKFORTON HILLS

A grim headache
squatting on its ridge,
black spider brooding
on a history
of arrows, boiling oil;
spilt blood darkening its stones.

Winds carve crude weaponry
from rock — blade and saw-toothed edge.
A creep of trees advances
up one flank, birds cling
in the furious air
below its walls.

Charlotte Henson

FOSSIL

The soil peels back, hands us our wages
with dirty hands. Cool beside us, twenty miles north,
where cotton towns smoke our treasure,
women knit, plait, thread, lose a finger or three.

Men-turned-gasmasks step down
into the darkness. A black face
peers from the gas-heavy pit.
The two-fingered women dream in vain
of the diamonds we might stumble across.
We get on our hands and knees and crawl,
are careful what we spit for light;
the air is thick.
       No diamond is clean.

The night averts her eyes
and the rain dropped to the shingle,
sacrificed itself to the earth,
and said not a single thing.

Sarah James

MUSEUM OFFERING

Neuropteris hollandica
Upper Carboniferous, Westphalian B, Duckmantian Stage

Dead Latin filters through the outside cries
carried in from fields, parks, streets...

This fossil alters the shape of my palm.
Flesh moulds to its mineral hardness,
as its mitten leaves offer up past lives
dislodged from a Wigan roof shale.

The fern's veins thread through the cracked
stone, imprint their presence as mine shafts
have outlined our landscape: pitted
surfaces, that sense of old ground shifting.

No sign now of the hands which worked
those coal seams. Only some answers.
This fern's known the weight of growth
and darkness, how fragility hardens.

Soft cells reduced to skeleton strength,
its shape is still cast into rock millions
of shades of sunlight later. Movement
continues around it: hands touch, feet pace,

voices fill our fields, parks, streets...
I place this firm ground in my pocket.

Scott Thurston

The following texts are taken from two perambulatory poem-performances which I undertook with the artist Elizabeth Willow in Sefton Park and Otterspool Park in Liverpool.

DAWN REDWOOD
(from *Truthing the Ground*)

Like many things
We try not to begin
At the beginning
We begin
In the middle

This tree
The Dawn Redwood
Metasequoia glyptostroboides
is a living fossil, native only to
China, and until 1941 was
Considered extinct

It finds a better climate here
Makes itself
a quiet intensity
at the heart of the park

Wearing its roots on its trunk
Twisting strands overlap, turn —
Seeking downward into what?

Two hundred and thirty five million years ago we're in
A desert of red sandstone
Somewhere near the equator

Twenty thousand years ago we're under
Three kilometres of ice
Eighteen thousand years ago we're in a meltwater
Chaos

But this poem is not a
Root-book, a
World-tree,
With a tap-root
Down into history

We cannot get access to
These dark layers
Of the unconscious
Of geological time
Try as we might

The world is chaos
What we need is
Something connected
To anything other
And which must be
'collective assemblages of
enunciation'
spoken in unison

We evolve by 'subterranean
Stems and flows,
Along river valleys
Or train tracks
We spread like oil'

We try and say the past
The present, the future
We try and split human
From nature
We try and say good, bad

But it all blows by in the Triassic dust

Nature imitates human
Imitates nature — a bole of a tree that
Moves as if by dancing

We gain and lose this territory all the time

Human captures nature
Becomes human becomes
Nature captures human
Becomes nature becomes

A-parallel evolution

Scott Thurston

UPPER BROOK WATERFALL
(from *Truthing the Ground*)

> Is it no verse, except enchanted groves
> And sudden arbours shadow coarse-spunne lines?
> Most purling streams refresh a lover's loves?
> Must all be vail'd, while he that reads, divines,
> Catching the sense at two removes?

— George Herbert 'Jordan (I)'

Come let's cross
the River Jordan

a river valley
formed by
glacial meltwater
10, 000 years ago

Let's cross

Via the Jordan River
Border Terminal built in 1994
Between Israel and Jordan
For use by Israeli citizens
And foreign tourists
With the exception of
Palestinians

Hold my hand,
Let's cross
Catch the sense

In 1604 Puritan settlers
From Bolton
Leasing the land from
The Catholic Molyneuxs

Named this brook Jordan
The areas of their farms became
Known as the Holy land

Jeremiah Horrocks
Who observed the
Transit of Venus
Across the Sun in 1639
Was born at Jericho Lodge
In 1618 and died 23 years later
Downstream at Otterspool

No illusions here
Just cross
You have to get your feet wet
Catch the sense
At two removes

An albedo feedback
Starts to form
Over modern
ground covered by snow

Frozen snow
reflects almost all
sunlight falling on it
back into space
and therefore stays cold

But once the snow at
the edges starts to melt
dark ground emerges
which absorbs sunlight
and therefore gets warmer

Let's get over
This river

We need our enchanted
groves
and sudden arbours

Scott Thurston

OTTERSPOOL PROMENADE
(from *Treading Water*)

I. *The Monument*

We overlook the water's
edge —
glimpse the ships of the
Danish Viking Tóki
entering the Mersey
in the tenth century

They land in the inlet
name it Tóki-staith
or Tóki's landing place

In 1930, John Brodie,
the City Engineer,
oversees the construction
of this River Wall
and, behind it,
the tipping of
clean domestic refuse
and rubble
from the Mersey tunnel
to reclaim land

We are standing on
two million tonnes
of waste —
including an entire
steam train
which fell into the
liquid mud

The mayor praised
Brodie's work as
giving 'wealth from
waste, beauty from
ashes'.

In 1640
Horrocks was here
measuring the tides:

'the motion of the seas has indicated many rare things to
me… it is strongly regular but is subject to many variations
of motion and remarkable inequalities…The observations
so far have continued for three months. However, I hope if I
remain here for a whole year I may discover many secrets
which may openly prove the motion of the Earth'.

II. *By the River*

We need to attend to sea level
To high tide
To tread, mark water,
To truth it straight

The sea is rising,
interacting with
land still rebounding from
the ice

it warns us that
storm surges might
become more frequent,
that the global temperature
is rising

read aright it
conveys uncomfortable
messages
is far from eternal

is ever-changing
where once was
a desert of ice
a desert of sand

Horrocks too
examines the water's
movement to grasp
his world better

He tries to make
sense of the lingering
uncertainty he feels:

'some small discrepancy merely contingent and irregular
should be reserved for only the foresight of the creator, so
that man might not boast of any perfection, but by a limited
skill be taught modestly to esteem his own confined wit'

We have trod
down the gorge
of an ancient stream
now joining the
river
beneath our feet
            —   have we found our own level?

like an ancient glacier
we can now release
our pebbles —

for what has come downstream
let it
tread
water

'I made this song from the river,
sculpted it from wave and driftwood'

———————————————————

SALTWATER

The river's mouth is sewn up
to stop its ebb and tide, its perpetual pull,

bone dry, thick dry, rough dry

no more watery reach
beyond the horizon, and our days.

I am a mouth wide open
sucking up the city's sounds:

I need words to wash our wounds.

Every chant, every incantation
is a sod of soil, a heavy weight,

ingested into acid
into blood and marrow

until my stomach turns,
mouths up a fresh spring morning:

as the days rough over my tongue.
I lick my lips. I laugh.

I try to catch the words as they run
liquid into the clotting river,

a rainbow of oil on the surface of the water
a spillage, an eruption,

sliding over the surfaces
on the moon-hauled tides,
and out into the constant depths off shore:

the constant future
where suspended underneath the waves
inside the deep green silence

a seagull's wing beat,
or a motor's hum,

or the thud of the container's hull
moored up tight against the harbour wall,

wait for their return at the turn of the tide.

And that water is my own.
I also live inside it.

O hear me call
in the flux of sunlight.

I am not the dryness in the shadows.
I am not a cloudless sky.

I made this song from the river,
sculpted it from wave and driftwood.

O I am abundant and you are not.
Howl to the sea. Howl to the salt.

Steven Waling

LEANDER SWIMS THE MERSEY

terror pain or peril   how can there be
in the mind   so much water in the sky
of a person who is   safe but the Temple of
Leandro lost   Venus melts into mist

the Manchester marsh

outside enough   small against tempest
rainfall for a month   the sublime
between us   is sliding into myth
le gouffre   fearful abyss

look at that sky   in the knowledge
the Mersey's grey muscle   they were in fact
cars aquaplaning streets   subject to deluge
drains can't cope   covered in the rising

rivers of cotton Lancashire

jet stream can't shift   waves a boy lost
rivers burst their banks   in the whiteout
Ramsbottom   danger swims
Crawshawbooth   with Byron
down to the deltas
                                    the effect of greatness
to the Irish Sea   upon feeling
the Ribble the Lune   the Goyt and the
the Irwell the Medlock   Hyndburn
sluicing down the Fylde   gives him the ague

the rainsoaked plain

91

low pressure from the
East
spins round its axis
Hero falls to despair
I live by the river

swims down from the
hills
drowned as a man
attempting to reach
love's light on the shore

Michael Egan

THERE BY A JARG RIVER HE LET GO A JARG FLIM
after The Seafarer and The La's and Liverpool

I can make lies from songs
like the doledrums of melody
or memory are just words plucked
from some other la's lips
and how often have I endured,
not endured, enjoyed
walking down to the river,
not down to the river, walking
near the river and seeing
it, dusk stained and wide,
from the end of an avenue,
not an avenue, from the end
of a private estate, not a private estate,
from the end of a council estate
(delete this, there is not this
in rhyme, in skald slobbering)
and there are no tossing waves,
no there are no worries, no abodes
for worry, for curb sleeping worry,
just that it was the last flim I had, I held,
I barely held, and not enough for bifters,
and there it is now, tossed about
by terrible tossing waves, beneath sheets,
no not sheets, beneath a sky low and heavy
and fat with thunder, not thunder,
just the sound, not song, of low hulled barges
lazily leading lower hulled barges
to work, no not to work, not us,
and waking, later, listening to leftover
music, long lost music of dirty summers,
of decade gone summers,

the night's anxieties take me,
how it slipped away, a leaf,
a flimsy leaf, a flim taken
by a nearly river, a jarg river,
a river of untrustworthy currents,
a river barren of ships,
barren of cliffs to wreck ships against
and lacking the prows of ships,
no not prows, and lacking the prayers
of ships, no not ships, and lacking
the prayers of men who think
their hearts full of sorrow, their troublesome hearts,
and being silent then on and on.

Clare Kirwan

OVER THE WATER

On this side wading birds line up
evenly spaced: the usual suspects.

Over the water, new towers rise
with metal fists to summon clouds.

On this side, promenade centurions
patrol the river's battlements.

Over the water your turbines spin the wind
and windows shine like diamonds.

On this side we wave like abandoned aunties
you do not want to visit, who boast of your success.

Over the water all your new splendour
is a kind of puppetry suspended by cranes.

When I'm there I look back again to this side
when I'm here I look across to you,

seagulls polka dot the sky over the water —
like them I am lost somewhere between the two.

Pauline Rowe

GODDESS, WAITING

I know it comes each year, even here,
especially here — this wide estuary drowning
voices like mine, words that rattle through the sea.

I spit on tolerance, negotiation
any genre of diplomacy.

You think the light of morning preferable —
dry as a contemplative nun, or holy fool waiting
for his ship-mates, mewling on a platform without food.

You set a stage for me in a neat green field or park —
flabby, obedient, brimming with maternal sorrow, silent.

Wearing my skin loose and gathering flowers in it.

I'll starve myself to bone, howling up a storm of ice
inside the echo of the Irish Sea, kill every creature
that dares to scent my skirts.

I'll bargain any ransom for her quick return,
set the abundant fields on fire, delight to hear
the cries of farmers cracking dry with thirst,

stop the cool streams before they start,
turn back the promised rain and curse
the Lancashire plains with drought.

I'll destroy all that is good,
sweet, scented, beautiful, fruitful,
yellow-petalled, rain-blessed
unless, until I find my daughter

gather her whole and sighted
from that hidden place

reclaim her, from the lost,
joyful and untouched.

David Seddon

SOUGH

It breaks in us like artillery —
the welter and shelter and shell of the sea.
The dock gates straddle the years apart
and waves explode easterly.

You walk along a shoreline
packed with driftwood,
remembering things:
workshops, workhouses, factories,
Atlantic greyhounds.

The past and future are washed-up
on the sand:
a rusty tin of Manx kippers,
oil from the refinery,
threads of wool
and a cottonless bobbin
strangled in a nylon drift-net.
A soap box,
a burst barrel of cod.

You stare at stones
as if they were scree
loosened by Wordsworth's stride,
looking for revolution
or the end of The Trade
fracked by a drumstick.

Like a man salt-panning for gold
in diamond-encrusted football boots,
you dip a glass finger
into the pool, pull out

a museum ticket, a kiss-me-quick hat
a cloth cap
a silk purse
coal.

Andrew Forster

GRANGE-OVER-SANDS

This November Sunday we're the only ones
strolling past palms in the careful border.
Flowers have mostly gone but an odd splash
of red, drying to parchment at its edge,
shines from the shingle like an old flag.

The railway cuts in front of the town,
entry to this prom only through a tunnel
or white-gated crossing, but it was the train
first brought merchants to this fishing village
that even then seemed left behind,

reached mainly by coach across the sands
when the tide pulled the sea from the bay,
horses splashed over the estuary bed,
coachmen mapping a route where sands were firm
and streams shallow: many lost to shifting sands.

Now the River Kent, which flows into the bay
has altered course, and the prom stares out
on sheep grazing cordgrass, water reaching us
only though channels written in saltmarsh
like letters from a forgotten language.

On a bench, where a brass plaque remembers
someone else who loved this place, we gaze
at Arnside Knott, pan across to Morecambe.
When the light is right we can almost see guests
enter the white shimmer of the Midland Hotel.

We should grow old here, in this town
of terraces; merchant's houses matured
to hotels and nursing homes, looking down
waiting for the long-rumoured moment
when the Kent changes its course back.

'A footprint dabbed in drying concrete, a sharp breath on brick'

Evan Jones

CAVAFY IN LIVERPOOL

Here is your sad young man:
he is ship-to-shore, he is buttoned-down
in tweed and scarved, eyes closed
when the Mersey wind

calls his collar to his ear
on the strand near Albert Dock,
some January, some winter day
we recognize but take no part in.

Here is your boy at the end of the shore
while the waters continue
touching place and nothing,
hold something dear and don't,

the desire and devotion
to an island he never dreams.
Not summoned, not answered,
he searches the world growing dim

as the river swells and recedes,
like closed eyelids shifting during sleep.
One less wave, he thinks, one less,
and then the Persians can get through.

David Seddon

LIVER BIRDS

One looks out to sea,
the other protects its own.
Outwards and in. It's the way
of it here. On the tide
you're held and rocked,
load up, rise, leave. But
the sand-bar buoy,
the cat's eyes on the Thirwell
feel you coming and wink, make
the breeze bring you
home.

The chains don't tether
but bind and brace. Dream
and they carry you in their beaks.

IN UNADOPTED SPACE

> Have we asked enough questions about space
> and what surrounds space
>
> Michael Palmer

The Google Earth van trawls Nicander Road for fresh image, flaking the brittle brickwork, brushing the privet invaded by wild rose, elderberry. Politics enflows form into space. Rails track the heft and heave of lapping coastline, shoulders of obdurate cliff. Affect flows through space into form. Form is content. It matters how the matter of the poem is made. Poetics is space. Its spirit material, as is the earth's. Form.

Scraps of maps are plans we move with. Planes. The ocean bed sings.

The cat mewls inside the house. Outside, the train blasts the air with two tones in Doppler twists. Spirals and tense torquing in eddies. No homeostatic system. Walking at the edge. Of the body. Of territory, tapping our toes against extension. Wind funnelled between the sheer office blocks slapping our faces. There's room here for more than room, ambient knowledge: volume, continuity, stretch. Sphinx atop the concrete Corinthian column. Diurnal reports repeat don't repeat. Fog scrubs the Cathedral from the skyline, heaves a grey sigh of release. Building space inside space outside. Wherever you are, you are always. Somewhere else. The Google Earth van trawls Nicander Road for fresher image.

Chorus. The province barks at its own echo. He thinks with the city, measures plains, grassland, wilderness against it.

107

Look Out. Desert. Sections and connections are always everywhere. Else. The trees on the rise thrust towards the castle on its crest. Alignments and movements: rumbling and rambling. And the distances between talking and walking. The mountains threw themselves up behind that squat cottage, becks dropping helpless with scree, he sang.

Aural environments: fractal practicals at the border zones. Length, breadth, height: sand, shingle, waves. Hearing distance as salt whisper wiped by sea wind. Smelling dawn pollinating the air. Sensing dusk, dull with petrol-fumes, heavy with fatigue. The melancholy moan of a foghorn from the river, dis-located, low and long.

Global networks in touch. On Google Earth the cybernetic tramline pulls you down Nicander Road and swings you into Bromley Avenue, a woozy swerve. But the connection snaps, re-locates you to some other street in Liverpool, similar Edwardian pattern-book terraces. A non-strategic misfire, it still models a brain process we recognise. On Google Earth you could see me sitting at the window, at the corner, hunched over the desk I'm typing on now on the laptop upon which I have saved the still shot as proof, bled through with the logo of the lensholder. Undeletable. All the windows thrown open as depixellated pictures of clear sky. There's no tactic to avoid this. I'd better be me with all this around me within me.

What is the opposite of a map? Redacted space: black military establishments, scenes of midnight renditions, fault lines across the human covenant. Long-ago demolished buildings or streets, not even a name left. Prompts for your own hushed movement piece. You can piece it together, pull it apart. Re-form, distend, grasp. Running up the hill the granite buildings stretch for you to gauge height. No map is a poem. Ambulation as life, writing. The bus station twists its neck as you run past. Once you move, you're part of it. Radius, latitude, amplitude. Drums thunder in unison between the giant effigies. A bass drum spins in the air, is caught by the smiling girl as she dances

between the march's pulse. Lebensraum environ-
mentalism: De-selected Welsh village drowned in the
1950s. Leaving the tap running (now), brushing teeth,
spitting blood (here). There's no map of civilisation which
is not at the same time a map of barbarism.

At the edges of the edge the fabric rips. A crumbled bank
flakes soft tufts into the river, which sink, fog beneath
reflections of willow branches drooping from either bank.
The war between the betweens. On Google Earth you see
me sitting at the window in the 'near-suburbs'. So that's
where I am! We're everywhere, but somewhere (in there)
are limitless questions of outernationalism, as machine
guns stutter across invisible borders, ritual slurs between
rival uniforms. Forgotten spaces between within beyond
the Archipelago. Entwinings. Wires hoisted between
frames, dishes cupped towards the sky, domes throbbing
out of the earth. Whisper capture. Avoid in-dwelling
verticality: delimited space, squeeze. Take place.

But the centre of the old city emptied of people becomes
space again. Swept, spread, open to the sky, the earth
littered with crumpled material, utility lost. Sclerotic car
radiator, crippled supermarket trolley, an umbrella with
mangled limbs, torn skin. No one to breathe them into life.
On the edges, the spaces strain to achieve placehood.
Buildings clutch the ground for purpose, testing a face to
face down the world, trying on a bit of grandeur. Slap,
whitewash. Front. Trying to take root on the route.
Betweenness devalued, replete with emptiness, sentiment.
Foggy sediment.

Energies in the infosphere. Unstable and dehistoricised
intangibles: fossil fuels evaporate into mists of
mystification, clouds of apps. A two second flicker of Gothic
castellation in a corporate slide-show. Rigour in scope,
scape, 'field'. A word like 'value' devalued. Flow flux
flexibility: management-speak. Consultation, partnership,
participation, rather than small people gathering wet
timbers from the collapsed pier to cart off as firewood;

patience drying. Boundaries, borders, littorals; edges as necessities. The crunch of razor shell scallops on damp excremental sand. The elusive point of interruption to the flows. Only there can the spiralling, the jetting, the spinning, the twisting, the stretching, the interweaving, begin afresh.

Tensions set up. The body as a space, its impressions on and through space, extend into space, are burnt onto space, or into places. A footprint dabbed in drying concrete, a sharp breath on brick, an orgasm printed on black plastic sheeting, a great thought bouncing off plate glass. A gigantic retina curved over the city, awash with glimmers.

Contest all spaces. Trust the wrong map. Unfold it in high wind, its torn creases, its ripped sheets, shredding. The palimpsest we try to read under without writing over. Polished corridors, shaded, drip antiseptic light, on clear purpose.

Beyond the anti-pastoral of relished decline: white goods, dented and fringed with rust, verdant boxy computer monitors, tattered plastic bags of garden waste, mouldering bundles of newsprint. Skidding their surfaces, distances.

Resist poems as landscape, landscape as poetry. The stanza's roomy poetic. Jagged lines of granite with caesurae of glacial collapse as metre. With room for more than roomage, it's not clear how the spatial may be given. Loopy spray-can tags glimpsed (en route) in railway sidings. Unconvincing equivalence: letters drooping as the word drops.

No space is empty. Slithers of turf sliced from the ground, then coiled for sale, between here and there. Location as dislocation. Bodily space in geometrical geographical geological spacetime. Seeing is shaping: registering. Columns of turf-squares crowding one corner of the rectangular field. A still tongue yearns for the word lost from all languages that embodies the mingle of desolation, desire and elation, felt only here. Elbow room, room to swing a cat. Making this world, it's not a question of expansion muscling constriction; it's about reshaping, interrelating: unfinish. The obstruction — empty luxury apartments with silver balconies — becomes the View once the shimmer on the Mersey at sundown is forgotten, sinking fingers of light.

Nicander Road straight as a silver wire through thick forest by the Great Lakes. That's superimposition as (one) method. Finding surprise in the already contrived while tracing an obligatory route, another. Perform all human noises and all mechanical sounds in your head, between Moorfields and Sandhills stations. Every day. Call it music. The bleeping doors its limits. Listen! Burst into the light, the choppy estuary, the headland under low clouds, the observatory thumbing the open sea.

The Google Earth van trawls Nicander Road for freshest image. While unadopted space is gradually tarred, people walk a fresh trail through the grass. It tunnels, is written into the script of that day alone. Stems heal from the slant. Not only connect. Disconnect, dissolve. To be somewhere is nearly always to be somewhere else. Not nearly. That square at Florence was at Krakow too, he thought. Dwelling in shift. Don't just Occupy: Evacuate!

Dave Ward

FROM ... WHERE THE WORLD BEGINS

Sandy stands where the sea meets the river,
the river meets the land:
where these worlds merge — a no-man's land.

    Sandy is no-man.
    Sandy is everyone.

Sandy drifts dreaming on the Seventy-Two
down the tree-lined mile of Menlove Avenue,
riding out to the Priory
to collect his crust of bread
and his cup of luke-warm soup.

Then on to the turn-around at the Horses Rest,
beside gap-toothed headstones for long-lost pets,
cadging bacon and burgers
at the trailer in the lay-by.

This is where the sky begins.
This is where the city ends.
    But Sandy turns back —
back to the streets that taste of the sea.

    Old shopping precincts peel and decay,
    clapboard faces flaking,
    weatherworn and weary
        as mothers in headscarves
    tugging their kids, frantic in the wind.

Lost ghosts throng and wave
behind the high metal railings
of the gaunt nursing home on the corner,

calling and singing through tall grey trees,
hiding behind the dull shadows of leaves
where derelict summer-houses slither and rot.

    The Jewish cemetery at Springwood.
    White gravestones picked out in neat rows
    behind the black-chained fence.

Blundering back to the old drinking clubs:
Dutch Eddies, the Embassy, Gladray and Tun-Tum
pulsing all-night reggae rhythms
seeping into the veins of traffic
surging down Upper Parliament Street.

    The late-night Somali cafe.
    Silhouettes of old sailors sit
        hunched over dominoes
    in the window.

Shadows of Chinatown's Sunday morning market,
squawk of cockerels trapped in baskets.
Tall men in robes and pigtails
haunt the Nelson Street doorways.

By the side of the dusty dock road
an old woman in a purple coat
and make-up pale as the moon
presses against the bars of the fence,
clips strands of lavender straggling wild
and tucks them into her brown leather bag.

    Time travels.
    Time trawls.

Sandy sees it all.
Sees everything.
Sees nothing —
only the next unsold Echo, the empty cups of tea.

Sad and bedraggled, Sandy watches.
His coat hangs dull, the colour of dust.
Never sleeping, never waking.
He is always here.

Listen ...
    Listen ...
        Listen ...

Janine Pinion

DEPARTMENT STORE, 1965

It sounds like sand
but it's blood-red starred with gold.
And it isn't the *craic* of basalt baked
into a hard puzzle of cups and columns,
but a hushed theatre of carpet, tiers spilling
and quietening the grain.

It isn't the wind playing
a slot filled with sea-thrift
nor the urgent roll of boats docking and leaving,
but the warm breath of perfume sales and leather
and cloth folded cuff to hem.

This is late summer's rite: casting off
into soft hands and measures,
the year's skin shed
on a changing room floor.

They know the lie of bones, pressing
fingers into seams and chalking
allowances for growth. Smile.
My dress is a bell. Look
at my feet through the eyepiece
of the magic box — *I have become a skeleton.*

Across the aisle, worn shoes buckle
like shipwrecks, each hold a perfect footprint.
I move my toes like seaweed.

Lindsey Holland

THE PORT OF LIVERPOOL BUILDING:
MAY 3RD, 1941

The night of the direct hit, Jack is fire-watching
on the third floor. Smoke comes up the stairs,
through vents and floorboards, feels its way
to his nose and between his teeth.

He reaches the lift and — because of the dark
or the armload of documents obscuring his feet —
steps into nothing, lands on his back

in a rot of cables, old oil, shallow water,
the anonymous smell of forgotten crevices,
and the thought of that space above.

With his cracked vertebrae, shattered ankle,
one foot as straight as his tibia,
he hears the next man fall and heaves himself clear.

They drop in a pile. Each howls,
murmurs, grabs at breath and lets it slip.
He listens to the drip a few yards away.
Someone's jacket tickles his wrist

and he clings to a skyline: new silhouettes
of cranes and scaffolding. One day, very small,
he'll walk underneath, along the dock road,
and turbines will rise from the estuary.

Sheila Hamilton

FREQUENTING THE STANLEY PALACE
Chester

The *most haunted building* in Chester,
though whether by a Grey Lady
and a Headless Man
or a Headless Lady and a Grey Man,
no-one is certain.

Murmurings. Laughter.

We bring tangerines, notebooks.
We brush against the ruffed and ruffled,
the farthingaled,
the enamoured,
the plagued.

We sow new hauntings,
poems that chatter, gabble,
tumble over themselves,
poems that halt, stutter,
try again,

and downstairs, there is salsa, its beat and colour.

Pauline Rowe

A HOSPITAL REMEMBERS

I have held them digging in my open fields
deep foundations on the land, to build
a place of hospitality, for the city's sick.

I have battled against every ill —
smallpox, poverty, tuberculosis, war,
damp oppression, huddled city life —

some tormented, those frail with age,
women calling out, infants screaming
with new life. *First, do no harm.*

The thin bringing of soldiers tight with terrors
from the pits of France. Sent bombs
to burn my walls, civil servants to confuse me.

My best loved days in recollection see
the asymmetric sweetness of my apple trees —
how I nourished my children. My gentle, simple paths,

my dreams, in bluebell woods, of pioneers
who bring their gifts of mind and hand
to save us. How we recreate

few hopes of the sick and protect them.
This, here, our small town of healing
with love, with service, with our best endeavours:

God has given this peace to us. *

*Note: an inscription in the plasterwork of Fazakerley Sanatorium,
Liverpool

118

'A speech born in marl,
fashioned in clay,
caked in coal'

THREE CAFES IN NORTH-EAST LANCASHIRE

HELMSHORE TEXTILE MILL
(sample: William Hazlitt, *on Fashion*)

I finish my coffee   a feel of studied neglect
green chairs   wrapped confectionery fashion
exists only by being participated among

a certain number of persons   café tinkle
of polite conversation discussing a certain
standard   the water wheel loomed over

the fulling stocks boomed time   shrinking in
its urine wash   Watch the Derby Doubler
pull threads into line   it cannot be lasting

for it depends upon the thinnest of yarns
and shifting of its own harlequin   designs
born of nothing   begot of this valley

crammed as a weaver's arse   Starved
hands building roads the read and solid will
never do for the current coin   between

Burnley and Blackburn   walk famine roads
along the myth of the English   exclusion
its lodge deep enough   to drown in

WHALLEY ABBEY
(sample: William Hazlitt, *My First Encounter With the Poets*)

I'm sampling this rarefied air   red
rustling leaves of the sturdy oak trees
stones of the Abbey   all over my soul

has indeed took B roads through
the Pennines   ashlar in various churches
ruins echo   talk of English Heritage

line of communication tissue   of
misericords in the Parish Church
established   The Green Man made a

poetical and pastoral echo   by the
Calder the gossip of birds   I remember
past the Gate House   disappearing

like vapourish bubbles   gaps that were
windows long dissolved psalms   the
pilgrim route the ghost of song   a poet

was to my father a sort of no-descript
echo   psalms that were gaps   the jobless
singing hymns on street corners   crosses
scattered cloisters   rather nice fruit cake

TOWNELEY HALL, BURNLEY
(sample: William Hazlitt, *On Personal Identity*)

Coffee at the stables   and who are you
that ask the question   a battlement crow
ladies walked the long gallery   full of pious

and brave   turned into a flower a star
a precious stone   tenants plough his fields
as Richard measures rain   priest hole closed

we may sometimes find ourselves   envying
the great hall's plasterwork   my schoolboy neck
craned up to its mouldings   that soul is our

that sacred passageway   opus anglcanum
but the rising sigh is soon checked   recusant
birds shriek out of the gloom   damp woods

lemon cake with walnuts   if one was born
a lord   did I once step into these kitchens
time stitched our secrets into the fabric

of Abbey vestments   drizzle in the grounds
life would have been one long drawn sigh
this kind of weather   I reach the road where

a bus wakes me   a wagon wheel on the wall

Cath Nichols

MISS LYDIA RAWLINSON TAKES HER TEA WITH SUGAR
Lancaster

Have you read Mary Wollstonecraft? Her *Vindication
of the Rights of Man,* and now *The Rights of Women.*

These 'rights' she talks of — I cannot see why we need
                                              them.
We're all owned by someone, it is God's order: I belonged
to my father, he died. Now I belong to my brother,
this is the way things are, I have no objection ... Milk?

I'm glad, perhaps, to be free of a husband. My shares
in the business are one sixth, and though wealth ties me
to family, I prefer this bondage
to the one made through marriage.

Do you take sugar? Good, I am so pleased!
There are some fools who think that by refusing sugar
the market will collapse and the slaves will be freed.
Such nonsense! If the market fails the slaves

will be made homeless. My brother, Abraham, has written
on the subject. He says, *'Many have left off the use
of sugar for the purpose of putting a stop to the slave trade.
If the custom becomes prevalent of eating and using*

nothing *that has been touched by slaves, we may soon expect
                                    to see*
*people in the state of their first nature, naked in the field,
feeding like Nebuchadnezzar upon the grass'.*
He is right! How *can* we avoid cotton, mahogany, rum?
                                    They are

the clothes we wear, the chairs we sit on, the glass we raise.
Those people who take their tea and coffee bitter —
what kind of world are they trying to make? What next?
Will they drink their tea black, to show sympathy for the
                                                    cow?!

Who do they want to grow their tea and coffee?
Who do they want to harvest sugar cane?
White men? How much will a cup of coffee cost then?
We must trust our merchant brothers to do what is best

for the economy *and* for the slaves. What we Rawlinsons do
is essential for Lancaster and for Liverpool. Trade
has served us well; kept us comfortable. We cannot
stop now, too many people rely on our family's enterprise.

We shall not give in. Mary Wollstonecraft can spout
all she likes, this business is for the men to decide.

Note. Wealth from the slave trade built most of the public buildings in Lancaster and Liverpool. There are portraits of the extensive Rawlinson family in the Judges Lodgings Museum, Lancaster.

DEEP CUTTING

(1814 – 1826)
and the hill said
the slab stones said
         you made a hole in me
pickaxe navvy men
dynamite blast men
rumble crack pause then
all fall down again ...

... you made a hole in me

(1930 – 1960)
and the town said
the terraced town said
         you made a hole in me
shut down cotton mills
shuttle stop loom stills
dole queue red bills
jam bread belly fills ...
... you made a hole in me

(1950 –)
and I said
from the edge I said
         you made a hole in me
she falls and he goes
shipped off before it shows
can't keep it heaven knows
bootees with pink bows
hands her over doors close
but see, see ...
... you made a hole in me.

Dinesh Allirajah

THE IMPERFECTION OF LANGUAGE

the orchid does nothing to scatter its seeds
each one that drops from its solitary stamen
will become its neighbour
just as
this moment here between us
will pass
to someone else should you choose to tell of it

William Roscoe the poet
put down his pen and picked up his spade
after his wife died
flattered with hope
he founded the Botanic Garden
planting himself
in the new soil to grow again or perhaps burying
his loss
allowing silent colours scents and form
to raise fresh clamour

Edward Rushton the poet
for whose hands I substituted
and compensated for his lost sight
blinded in youth in a slave ship's hold
the only crew to make contact or offer care
to the shackled cargo
infection tunnelling through their eyeballs
into his
he could wear his affliction
to shame
those who came into contact with slavery
and did not also go blind

he gave me this to tell
a scribe in his employment
no longer required when his blindness eroded
and the crystallised fruit syrup air
to which his sight returned
was filled with trumpet petals and fragrant tongues
in Roscoe's garden he saw an orchid
belonging no longer to its home soil
it possessed this light residing here
among poets
who neither belong nor possess
he planted
the poetry of the moment in my ear
I whisper it to you

John Lindley

ELLESMERE PORT

Perhaps flat Manc' vowels
bubble beneath the surface of the Ship Canal,
Belfast brogue filters through the estuary,
Brum comes up from the 'Shroppie'
and hard Scouse consonants
wash from The Mersey as silt
but here it's all rinsed into something other —
other than even Birkenhead and Bebington,
Chester and Childer.

A speech born in marl,
fashioned in clay,
caked in coal,
greased by oil
and smelted as ore
speaks of its birthday —
remembers the stove pipe hats,
the high timbered ships,
the knuckles and spades
that cut the link from the Mersey to the Dee,
that dug for an idea
and uncovered an identity

and what was river speak, sea talk,
northern dialect and Cheshire tongue
is now an accent blasted from phenol
and buffed by a bar of three-penny soap
into the lyric of the land,
the lilt of the sea,
the patter of the Port.

RAGGEDY SCHOOL

Our beds are straight and white,
neat as matchsticks against the wall.
At night I pull covers over my head,
breathe my own breath, move my lips
into the shape of once upon a time.

Then dreams appear; odd weavings
of make-believe scented with oranges,
spectres dressed in whisperings
and fond names. Morning comes
pricking the calm with her sharp bodkin.

We are twenty sisters at the table,
tightly wound bobbins, forty scrubbed
hands, yards of neat hems. We beg
forgiveness, crave to be blessed. We are
one voice in an Institute's dress.

John Calvert

THE WATERS ARE FREED

We trail round the lake to a goose lament
Between apt showers
Old industries let slip waters thread
Unsluiced, the Etherow
Plunges from the screen of its fall
To the churning pool
Vortex brown and frothed
Like the beer we drink
Remembering our mothers
Slowly spinning away

Emma McCourty

A VIEW FROM THE TOP
Accrington Factory Bottoms

People loom
all day on machines
straining extremities
to fashion nylons
and blouses.

Loud orders crack
through stuffy air,
heralding work for
stiff, pin-pricked hands.

Silent in a crowded space,
women lace handkerchiefs
and nightwear
from daylight's first speck.

From the top of the hill
dog walkers stare across
to a view
of voluptuous clouds.

If they looked down
through shields of glass
they might see
the shadows of women
scrunch-backed,

fingers tender,
backs arched
and aching
over garments
they'll never wear.

Edwin Stockdale

MARDALE

The landscape is static
once scoured by slow-moving
boulders caught in ice.

Today the reservoir is low.
Remains of slate walls
protrude above the waterline.

Buzzards wheel in the sky
unaware of the bodies that were shifted
from the now-drowned village.

RAVENGLASS & ESKDALE RAILWAY

Steam shimmers
from River Mite's engine,
red as iron ore.

Beside Barrow Marsh
she startles oyster catchers.
Further down, by the water-mill

ringed plovers rise.
Rowan trees form an arch
and a red squirrel scrambles.

At the passing place, the River Esk
is black as coal-dust.
Saddleback pigs snort, turn away.

The River Mite continues,
hugging the bracken-clad hillside
watched by Herdwick sheep.

Reaching Dalegarth, she stops
as Northern Rock pulls out
in Muscat green livery.

Steph Pike

FORGED

urban alchemy
brick walls slur with liquid steel
the hills, clenched like fists, circle,
sheep-studded and angry
the sun a bullet hole in the sky
the city cries ice rain
hot and hard as rivets

'See the common medlar drop of its own accord.

See, once again, the knives in the porcelain sink'

Daniele Pantano

VAUDEVILLE

See the butcher's son lose faith in his knives.

See the worn dock line chafe against the pier.

See the scholar drag her desk into the woods.

See the finger cramp the penultimate étude.

See the grocer highlight his name on the front page.

See the truant child decide on a different shortcut.

See the seamstress enter the building for the last time.

See the survivor hesitate before a shop window.

See the common medlar drop of its own accord.

See, once again, the knives in the porcelain sink.

Andrew Oldham

TWO THOUSAND YEAR STARE

Glass vision; turned over in chocolate soil,
the boy who bought penny sweets is still
running down coffin ginnel, hollering,
with hand in crook of arm, barrelling

through a game of soldiers,
shoulders stuttering between mouthfuls
of warm caramel, that trickles down his chin,
pushing forwards and outwards through coffin end

into streets that are seasons.
Spring Street: he lurches, balloons
between the thighs of his daydreams,
tosses wax lips at neighbourhood kids,

jumps down across the potholes into
Summer Street: he runs, wind
in hair without a care of grenades,
his hand moving fast and sharp, sniping

through cracks in the boarded up houses on
Autumn Street: where the eaves are camouflage brown
and all the doors are painted khaki, blasting holes
in the cinder block macadam and net curtains

that twitch, like the wings of angels, carry him up
Winter Street. Not a house left, just holes
in the ground, a crossword puzzle of
two ups and two downs.

Alison Chisholm

ON THE BRINK

Our street was one-sided — every house was odd
for where the even houses should have been
parallel lines of road on road stretched forever
to the magic land of cake shops, bus stops, playground.
Our corner shop had fresh-sliced bacon, tea, canned
                                              peaches,
jars pink with spearmint, primrose with sherbet lemons.
At three I stood on the counter, danced and sang,
was rewarded with chocolate. Flagged pavements
throbbed with dog-walkers, stop-for-a-gossipers,
ice-cream-van-chasers, back-to-school-foot-draggers.

On the cusp between war and swinging sixties
we knew we were on the brink ... though no-one guessed
                                              why.
In the next street, the street after, the street after,
Adrian Henri was picking up a paintbrush,
Roger McGough was picking up a biro,
John Lennon was picking up a guitar;
and just beyond the streets after that
the swelling Mersey shifted, prepared
to change the rhythm of the world forever.

V. A. Sola Smith

PUNCH LINE

Tin tin tin, get it
or a eawl-leet skryke, t'be sure.
Every beggin' sennet down't pop shop, Pa Yammerin.
Tin tin tin is the ring o'life on't strap,
naymind scraps; Mam'll fix bally anne. Our kid,
tin tin tin, get it now, or 'cross Pa's lap,
a wisecrack, t'be sure;
the punch line's its own joke.

Andrew Taylor

4TH NOVEMBER 1978

    Oggy's Dad the coalman
has a real fire to this day

the city centre train takes sixteen minutes

    the ferns are out in force
first carriage deodorant artificiality

If you steal be Robin Hood

in this heat the washing will
    dry quickly

Idents barely out of black and white
    corner box a world away

Colour reproduction prototype
    video games

Dana says her braces are clear
    it is pointless photographing them

Deak's Dad ran a mobile shop
    during the bread strike

he'd bring loaves over for the kids

David Tait

SELF-PORTRAIT WITH TERRACED HOUSES

Time for goodnight:
and I can't believe
I'm being spun
like a bookstand
and pulled
to your lips
my crotch
to your crotch
our kiss.

This is not
that sort of town,
though how
to resist
when streetlamps
are glaring
and windows
straining
their blind eyes.

Soon the milkman
the paperboy
the morning commute

but now your hands
round my waist
streetlamps as searchlights
our kiss:

then this
        and this
                and this
                        and this

144

Alicia Stubbersfield

IN NEED OF SOME UPDATING

This was my house with the red-tiled porch
my mother polished with Cardinal not very often,
where swallows returned year after year,
fledglings bulging over the nest edge
inches from our back door. The water-tower
like a fairy castle beyond the garden,
next to the railtrack where Huskisson was killed
by Stephenson's *Rocket* on its first trip.

The house where I didn't contradict
and learned spellings for a test on Friday,
read pony books and kept myself to myself.
My bedroom at the front with the window
covered by a Venetian blind after I climbed out
to talk to the milkman's horse.

In the kitchen chutney bubbled,
Granny spoke Spanish or Scottish
and all the sadness was held at bay.
Here my mother made my mini dresses,
one a week for 60s discos and copping off
by ten o'clock, Cherry B or Babysham,
and knowing what nice girls didn't do.

I find it for sale on Right Move,
take the 360 degree virtual tour.
I'm not there in the dining-room
watching telly, my mother isn't sewing
at the kitchen table, my father is not telling
my mother to leave him alone
as he crumples on the hall floor
where I am no longer crying inconsolably
when the cat is lost, a year after he died.

Jan Dean

28 HANOVER STREET

Three sisters wait upon their father
— a despot much admired for living long —
wound tight in each other's skein
one keeps house, two work.
Time ticks. Shrinks them.
The leading edges of De Havillands
become the cogs and spools
of tame domestic stuff.
Hilda plays mother to her sisters
Mary reads romances
and Annie glowers
slaps down the nonsense
keeps the rent book
burns the billet doux
receives the tipped up wages
nips things in the bud.
Men who might have split the trio
prove fickle, die in convoys,
come nowhere near to measuring up.
Hilda is the first to go.
Nephrons — frilled and delicate
as fine lace doileys — inflame and fail,
Mary's solid knot of headache grows
like basalt in the brain,
now Annie sits at the edge of the room
rehearsing and rehearsing
a long list of wrongs
the stroke having stilled for ever
the whip hand.

Angela Topping

THE COMFORT OF HIDING
12 Black Denton's Place, Widnes

This oak roof comforts me whenever
Mother drives the hoover monster close;
I see its snarling metal teeth. The house is
my own address, my damask walls.

Under this table, I have kissed feet:
they are gone now, these people I love.
It's just me and my doll, and she
is no company at all. Her eyes are empty.

When my mother's house is full again
I will emerge, be given sweets. My daddy,
home from work, will invite me
to sit in my other place, the house he makes

between his back and his chair's back.
I do not know why hiding is needed
or why when I'm sad I go under the bed
where balls of grey dust scut like rabbits.

Andrew McMillan

NOT QUITE

each of us having loved each of us

in some earlier room of our lives

there was the awkward intimacy

which only comes from having grasped

between our lips the truest part

of one another   and now the task

of the bedroom   re-hung and altered

pick your euphemistic metaphor

stubbled sandpaper   the saw   shoulder

crowning weight of lifting a settee

arms we touched seeming to grow towards

our hands as though our hands were light

the mirror   watching ourselves undress

'how fast the weather changes

how fast the roofs become summits   streetlights
                                           stars'

Andrew Taylor

THE SOURCE THAT THE BRAIN PREFERS

Hollisters attempt a cover-up
    previous hipster leggings
rucksack partner hand holding
    Cali looks

    branded escalator
travel the northern line

flip flops in the rain

ad candidate
    take the blanket
    take the cup
    take the alcohol

like Tiffany
    the season's hottest mix

is this a story of passion
youth and love of the sea?

harmony of romance
    beauty adventure

Natural tones minimal make up
    Southport is not in California

Blank hoarding the joy of not being
sold anything

at all

the rucksack is wide open

151

WHEN WIDNES WAS IN LANCASHIRE
AND I WAS IN WIDNES

I climbed my childhood scrapheap,
finding footholds on old prams,
rusting bikes; reddened metal
that slid under my feet and hands.

My fingers stretched to scrape the sky,
head buoyed up with words I'd claimed
understood but couldn't say
from all the books I'd hefted home.

The small town couldn't hold me. I
was Alice in Wonderland, stuck
in the White Rabbit's house, drunk
on grow-me potion, glugging it down.

The Transporter's comforting boards
upstaged by the dizzy arc of a bridge:
a monochrome rainbow, an exit sign
spanning the horizon, lit up in chemical dark.

From downriver, mermaids called me
to where the Mersey became the sea,
a gull-haunted strait with looming ships
to New Brighton, Éire, The Caribbean.

I was waiting for the wind to change,
to tread the yellow brick road
journeying beyond myself, beyond the town
beyond the people I had known.

Stephen Beattie

SOUTHPORT GENERAL 5AM

As the nil by mouth day
seeps through thin curtains
she stands beside my bed
marker pen poised.

With cartographer's precision
she inscribes lines
of longitude and latitude
on my stomach.

Slightly to the right
she draws a one inch circle:
just in case.

Later, surfacing from morphine's
greedy sleep,
I find the map redrawn.
Stapled ridges rise jagged
under gauze snowcaps:

slightly to the right,
raw and rose coloured,
an island has emerged.

Just off its south shore,
etched in italics, are the words,
Here be demons.

NORWICH TO LIVERPOOL

I see red-brick terraced houses stacked
over the hill. Occasionally complete strangers
say hello in the street. I could walk down

to the café in Anglia Square, dip a glazed bun
into a pyrex cup of weak tea and you'd come
flooding back. I could change at Crewe

and carry on north. I'd be looking for a time
as well as a place, but I doubt you still have
stockings drying on the fire-guard, wolf whistles.

I know you can buy souvenirs
and expensive coffee down at the docks
and you too, have a cathedral to spare.

JT Welsch

EX-PAT ON A NORTHERN TRAIN

Do I feel more or less foreign
passing an endless camper dealership
and finding, among the endless rain,
a field of camper-shaped sheep?

What a sheltered life you lead!
So says the guy who stole my girl
in high school. So says his dad,
who sheltered a night last week in jail.

Their rott died and he figured poison,
dealing directly with a shepherd neighbor.
They'd be at home here, father and son,
if it weren't for all us foreigners.

Kim Moore

TRAIN JOURNEY, BARROW TO SHEFFIELD

Even though the train is usually full of people
I don't like, who play music obnoxiously loud
or talk into their phones and tell the whole carriage
and their mother how they're afraid of dying
even though they're only twenty five,

even though the florescent lights
and the dark outside make my face look like
a dinner plate, even though it's always cold
around my ankles and there's chewing gum
stuck to the table and the guard is rude

and bashes me with his ticket box,
even though the toilet smells like nothing
will ever be clean again, even though
the voice that announces the stations
says Bancaster instead of Lancaster,

still I love the train, its sheer unstoppability,
its relentless pressing on, and the way the track
stretches its limb across the estuary
as the sheep eat greedily at the salty grass,
and thinking that if the sheep aren't rounded up

will they stand and let the tide come in, because
that's what sheep do, they don't save themselves,
and knowing people have drowned out there
like the father who put his son on his shoulders
as the water rose past his knees and waist and chest

and rang the coast guard, who talked to him
and tried to find him, but the fog came down,
and though he could hear the road, he didn't know
which way to turn, but in a train, there are no choices,

just one direction, one decision you must stick to.
This morning the sun came up in Bolton and all
the sky was red, and a man in a suit fell asleep
and dribbled on my shoulder till the trolley
came round and rattled loudly and he woke up
with a start and shouted *I've got to find the sword.*

Andrew McMillan

NEITHER HERE NOR THERE

startling   how fast city becomes hill

roads become tracks   how fast the lightglint

of sun on a 'scraper window is waterbounce

how fast the siren's wail is the mating chelp of grouse

people not people but oddly cast shadows

how fast the clouds run over

how fast the slow groan of plane reaches us

how fast the blue of one team becomes the sky   the red of
                                                       another

sky also   but a different time of day

how fast the weather changes

how fast the roofs become summits   streetlights   stars

how fast the birds   the bending plants   the neighbours
                                                       chatter

how fast two hundred square feet of living space seems
                                                       small

how fast   too   the heart becomes unfixable

and you lay your purgatoried body

neither here nor there

Jan Dean

ESCAPE SEQUENCE

A mallard glossy green
his mate neat as a tweed cushion
sit on the bank of the A50.
On the airport roundabout rabbits
all bounce race and white-scut
a stone's throw from *The Romper* —
      wooden lion, gold painted
      mane stiff in the winds' backwash.
Early Sunday by the NatWest bank
a sparrowhawk takes down a pigeon
and the blackbird's song
cuts no ice with the magpies
they do what they do.
The ducks move on.

Andrew Rudd

JOURNEY

She flips down
the indicator stalk
with her left thumb,
turns into the slip road
sees how it is:
no escape from this
slow river

into which
she must slide.
Between two lorries
a space declares itself
so she sighs into place,
jigsawed among grinding
and red lights,

a dark suburb
of disturbed slumber.
I call out
to my children
when I wake in the night
even though they are asleep
and it's all quiet

yes
I hate that journey
every day it's the same
the motorway, the lights
nothing to stop you thinking
what you don't want to think
you can't help it.

All this torrent
lurches, stops, abandons
all flow and rhythm
in awkward surges.
From vast distances,
the next junction and
the next junction call.

‘ ... we shall be
wild garlic memories before we know it.

I think of you, though we may not speak’

———————————————————

Janet Rogerson

FOREVER UNFAMILIAR

We were always lost
looking for International 2.
In whoever's arms

in Band on the Wall,
appraising surfaces
talking like noodles.

The eyes were dancing
in the Hacienda,
no really, they were.

We were lost
looking for the Apollo,
then the goats,

the first, unremarkable
then more, then everywhere,
sticking their beards

into everything.
Then you, like Vicious
slinking down

the steps in *My Way*.
We were lost looking
for International 2

the snow was lost too
swirling confused lost
I love you lost.

John Siddique

I THINK OF YOU

This year I reclaimed the 'Spring Wood'.
I haven't walked there since it was ours.
It's the same place, the huge rocks placed
down by glaciers before we knew anything.

We're as temporary as the bluebells
that come up in springtime, we shall be
wild garlic memories before we know it.

I think of you, though we may not speak,
though I go out of my way not to see you.
I think of you in a before it all happened way.

I love the bluebells growing in the green,
the permanence that each rock assures us of,
I think of you,
the green of the wood,
the bluebells and the stones.

Kim Moore

BEING MARRIED

We swear we'll never be like those couples
who say hello together, in a sing song voice,
the same pitch and timbre, we'll never buy
coats of the same shade and walk through
Windermere in the rain, or lift our matching
suitcases onto a train, I'll never go climbing
in the Isle of Skye just to please you, you won't
listen to my poetry unless you really want to,
we'll stay as separate as two cities must stay,
one trading in metal, the other in tourism.

David Riley

WALKING TO SOUTHPORT

If we were to stroll among the gull sirens
to reach the stiletto of Ribble
at low tide, it would take forever.

I glance at my shoes,
standing on the dust of mountains,
once proud. I look at her.
We decouple, walk slowly back to the shore
abandoning adventures again.

Andrew Oldham

THE LAST TIME WE MET

you tell me how hollow you are —
how no marriage, prams, high chairs and nappies
can plough furrows instead of laughter lines
you no longer paint
but sit in landscapes staring at far off hills
rubbing oils into your naked body
you have become dangerous in galleries
you need to be the exhibition
the yoke of the gilt frame
stretched, straining around your neck
your world has tightened and withered in a frame
when we part, I watch you leave
but you get lost in the crowd
crossing to the station
once a face I knew so well
shrinks easily among the commuters.

Rosie Garland

WALKING TO CASTLERIGG

He demands each detail of the walk: the splinter
of dried-out heather, the fly agarics clenched
in crimson fists, tea staled
by the thermos, the gravelly biscuits.

His face hangs above the mottled bedspread,
fingers fumbling for loose threads
in the weave to hang onto, haul
himself closer. His back hooks a question mark.

What we are not saying thickens,
promising rain before evening.
If there were trees here, I could read the landscape:
could track my way back by the gaps
between their outstretched arms,
the deep red wooden hearts of them, grounded.

'I am a structure
in the teeth of it'

———————————

A PIECE OF A FUTURE

He bounces past Scholes-Henge
wearing the uniform he slept in,
eyes sparking, spitting threats to no-one
through sugar-puff teeth.

Last night he was down by the duck pond,
necking vodka and slicing the tops
from ripples with stones.
Today, Miss writes 'Irreversible Reactions'
on the SmartBoard
while he carves his name into a gas tap.

Vandalism — an attempt to make a mark:
initials on a desk,
torn up exam papers,
wiping a smirk from a face with a brick.
Community cuffs and 'Assault' is added
to a steadily swelling Word doc.

You can catch someone every day
and still find no grip,
like molten iron spittering
from one broken mould into another.
Year 10 and no thin ice left to slip through.

So a future is forged, solid
as a sovereign ring
in someone's teeth, inevitable
as a trip and a curb-split skull.

Lights out
and he'll be there —
sleeping in uniform again.

BORDER

When he did go south, it was with a reluctant
and suspicious step, with his ear cocked
to the wind, ready for the first trace
of a clipped accent, the first slight
that knotted the muscles inside his coat.

He spoke as little as possible, just enough
to get supplies and if asked to repeat himself,
he'd roll the words around his mouth, spit them out
and then point, as if it were obvious.

When home, he'd put down his load,
sit before the fire to calculate
the benefits of a strong currency.

Matt Fallaize

ARGUABLY A HORIZON

Your earth's curvature
sees its sun sink
ten full minutes before mine
looking out

over glacial till the arks
of houses lost to the moss
reclaiming and climbing
barns sinking rotting stone

tilth and mere the
flatlands absorb no matter
how much history
how much narrative
they simply absorb

you had your neck craned back
saw suggestions of hills
imagined a riot of a climb
imagined a great day out

and though I watched towns subsumed
my sun set later

CLOWBRIDGE

The trees don't want to touch.
Fattened sheep rub their wool
against the hawthorn, cure that life-long itch;
crows labour in the wind like paper bags —
the battered landscape claims them. I run around in the
                                        mist
in my red coat while he keeps his eye on me, while the
                                        wind
stirs and dissipates like someone moving quickly away.
The trees do not mingle with their own kind; they bend
with the shape of the wind like an arc, a miser's spine —
as it bellows. There's a bridge over a tiny river by a house
where the water once churned in a turret and carried to the
                                        reservoir.
The cold smarts my chapped cheeks. In between my legs it
                                        burns.
The dog is swimming in the freezing water, I want it to
                                        drown.
I want the little boats on the water to capsize.
This place is bones.

AMOUNDERNESS

A grey grind spit,
the biggest sky
 wheeling and skirling
and cloud massing and remassing,
racing,
pulled by wire,
a taut line ribboned.
Strata of sun
and horizon
and gunmetal shining
and sand.
The one tall thing:
I am a structure
in the teeth of it,
forward leaning,

worn to a rind,
caddised in salt,
jaw cased
I do not shatter

We built knowing
If we stepped too hard
or carried too much
it would drink us.
 Water already pools around my foot,
a pale thing
freckled by mud,
with oval bits of sky
its childish outline.

I grit and re-grit
scouring skin
the smell of fish-rot,

floating things
all
reflecting sky,
catch a silvering from my
eye's corner
periphery flash
and no point in grasping
(though it's reflex)
see, the hands arc,
a useless poling as it fletch on nothing.

This place is the grist
the un-peace in my gut
the itch where my ribs meet
and tingles in my feet and hands
this is the low root of it,

a moan that scratches
and fills me
eyes half shut
and it is
both pleasure and pain
rocking slightly,
with the tide of breath,
with the current of a pulse,
sea drenched.

BIOGRAPHIES

DINESH ALLIRAJAH is a short story writer and jazz poet, born in London to Sri Lankan parents and based in Liverpool since 1985. He co-founded Liverpool's Asian Voices Asian Lives writers and performers' collective, and has performed and given workshops around Europe and in Bangladesh and Nigeria. His collection of short stories, *A Manner Of Speaking* was published by Spike in 2004. Individual pieces have appeared in several anthologies, including *The Book Of Liverpool* and *Re-Berth* (both Comma Press, 2008) as well as broadcast on BBC Radio 4 (March 2008). http://realtimeshortstories.wordpress.com/

ANTHONY ARNOTT lives in Ormskirk, Lancashire. His first collection, *Behind Barcodes*, was published by erbacce-press in August 2011. For two years, he was a Poetry Editor for *The Black Market Review*. He has also had work published in *Peggy's Blue Skylight, First Edition Magazine, Question Mark, The Journal, Streetcake Magazine, Why Vandalism? Journal, Broken Wine* and others, as well as in anthologies such as *The Strand Book of International Poets 2010* and *Liquid Gold.* A keen reader, Anthony has read in support of Jerome Rothenberg.

RICHARD BARRETT lives and works in Salford. His collections are *Pig Fervour* (The Arthur Shilling Press, 2009); Sidings (White Leaf Press, 2010); *A Big Apple* (Knives Forks and Spoons Press, 2011); and # (zimZalla, 2011). He can frequently be heard reading his work at events across the UK. Richard founded and now co-edits the innovative poetry magazine and press Department. There have 5 issues so far and three full-length collections.

STEPHEN BEATTIE was born in Lincolnshire in 1957. He has had a wide range of life experiences including work on a deep sea trawler, factories and public service. In 2005 he enrolled on a poetry course at his local college and has since had competition success and work published in poetry magazines in the UK and USA. His first collection, *Treading The Helix,* is published by Indigo Dreams.

ELAINE BOOTH-LEIGH lives in Wigan. Her poems have appeared in a number of anthologies including the Best of Manchester Poets 2. Elaine runs the Wigan Stanza group and regularly organises events at the Leigh and Wigan Words Festival.

JOHN CALVERT is a writer, musician and performer based in Manchester. He has published one book of poetry and a new volume is forthcoming from erbacce-press. He is currently working on a first novel, and the genesis of a major theatre work, *Rhydwnwyn, the opera.*

ALISON CHISHOLM writes regular poetry columns in *Writing Magazine* and *Springboard*, and has written instructional, humorous and autobiographical articles for magazines, radio and newspapers. Author of ten collections of poetry, a poetry correspondence course and a range of textbooks about the craft of writing, she has taught creative writing in adult education for 30 years, and gives readings, talks and workshops around Britain and overseas.

SARAH CORBETT grew up in North Wales and studied at Leeds University, UEA and Manchester University. She has published three collections of poetry with Seren Books, *The Red Wardrobe* (1998), shortlisted for the TS Eliot and the Forward First Collection prize, *The Witch Bag* (2002) and *Other Beasts* (2008). Sarah has just finished a verse novel and is currently writing a new collection of poems. 'To Scale' is from a new sequence that explores family and early life in the village of Saughall, near Chester. Sarah teaches Creative Writing for Lancaster University and lives in West Yorkshire with her teenage son.

DAVID J. COSTELLO lives in Wallasey, Merseyside, and is co-organiser of local poetry venues 'Bards of New Brighton' and 'Liver Bards'. His work has been published in several anthologies and poetry journals including *Quantum Leap*, *Reach Poetry*, and *Envoi*. He has been short-listed and placed in various competitions, most recently being short-listed for the Grist Poetry Prize and winning the 2011 Welsh Poetry Competition.

JAN DEAN has worked as a Poet-in-Schools for 25 years. She is widely anthologised and has two collections of poetry for children. She was born in Blackburn, brought up in Stalybridge, and now lives in Cheshire.

MICHAEL EGAN is from Liverpool. He runs Holdfire Press and Villainelle Poetry Club. His first collection, *Steak & Stations*, came out in 2010 from Penned in the Margins. He has had four pamphlets published. Recently poems have appeared in *The Forward Book of Poetry 2012*, *Adventures in Form*, *Lung Jazz* and *Best British Poetry 2012*.

CHRIS EMERY lives in Cromer with his wife and children. He is a director of Salt, an independent literary press. He has published two previous collections of poetry, a writer's guide and edited editions of Emily Brontë, Keats and Rossetti. His work has been widely published in magazines and anthologised, most recently in *Identity Parade: New British and Irish Poets*. He is a contributor to *The Cambridge Companion to Creative Writing*, edited by David Morley and Philip Neilsen. His latest book is *The Departure*, shortlisted for the EDP/Jarrold East Anglian Book Awards.

MATT FALLAIZE is a writer and chef living in Ormskirk, Lancashire, where he dishes out meals, stories and poems in uneven quantities. His first collection of poems, *L39* is available from Erbacce Press, and work has appeared in Stride, Neon Highway and Erbacce magazines, along with various webzines, anthologies and the Oulipo issue of Ekleksografia. A member of the Edge Hill poetry and poetics research group, another chapbook will hopefully be forthcoming soon from the Knives, Forks and Spoons press, provided he can get his damn finger out.

MARTIN FIGURA is a photographer, poet, retired Army Major and winner of the 1976 RAPC Apprentice College Accountancy Cup. He is part-time Finance Manager for Writers' Centre, Norwich and Chair of Café Writers. His Collection *Whistle (Arrowhead Press)*, together with the stage version, was shortlisted for the Ted Hughes Award for New Work and he won the *2010 Hamish Canham Prize*. The pamphlet *Boring The Arse Off Young People (Nasty Little Press)* also came out in 2010. He's performed his work from New York to Cromer and is a member of the Joy of 6 spoken word group.
http://www.martinfigura.co.uk/

ANDREW FORSTER has published two collections of poetry with Flambard Press: *Fear of Thunder*, shortlisted for the Forward Prize for Best First Collection in 2008, and *Territory*, focusing on the landscape of South West Scotland where he then lived. His poems are featured on the AQA GCSE syllabus. He worked as Literature Development Officer in Dumfries & Galloway before moving to Cumbria to work as Literature Officer with the Wordsworth Trust. This move influenced his most recent project, *Digging*, a pamphlet of new poems with accompanying drawings by the artist and printmaker Hugh Bryden, and published by Roncadora Press.

ROSIE GARLAND was born in London to a runaway teenager. She has always been a cuckoo in the nest. She is an eclectic writer and performer, ranging from singing in Goth band The March Violets, to her alter-ego Rosie Lugosi the Vampire Queen, twisted cabaret singer, electrifying performance poet and emcee. She has four solo collections of poetry, and her fifth, *Everything Must Go* (Holland Park Press) is out in July 2012. Her award-winning short stories, poems and essays have been widely anthologised. She has won the DaDa Award for Performance Artist of the Year, the Diva Award for Solo Performer, and a Poetry Award from the People's Café, New York. Most recently she won the Inaugural Mslexia Novel Competition and her debut novel *The Palace of Curiosities* has been picked up by Harper Collins.

GERALDINE GREEN is a Cumbrian poet who has read and been published in the UK, USA, Italy and Greece. Her poetry has been translated into Romanian and German. Green's collections are *The Skin* and *Passio* (Flarestack 2003 and 2006), *Poems of a Molecatcher's Daughter* (Palores Publications, 2009) and *The Other Side of the Bridge* (Indigo Dreams, 2012). Her next collection, *Salt Road*, also by Indigo Dreams, will be published in the summer of 2013. Green has a PhD in Creative Writing from Lancaster University, is a Visiting Lecturer at the University of Cumbria, works as a freelance creative writing tutor and mentor and is Associate Editor of Poetry Bay. www.poetrybay.com

SHEILA HAMILTON's poems have been widely published. She has had two pamphlets published, *The Monster in the Rose Garden* (Flarestack, 2001) and *One Match* (Original Plus, 2010), and a full-length collection, *Corridors of Babel* (Poetry Salzburg, 2007). She has lived in various places in England and Scotland, also in Hungary for two years where she taught English. She currently lives on the Wirral with her family and cats.

CHARLOTTE HENSON is a young poet from Greater Manchester. She is widely published and her work has appeared in several publications including *Cuckoo Quarterly*, *Blankpages* and *Best of Manchester Poets*. She is the sole editor of *Astronaut* magazine and her first collection *Pharmacopoeia* was self-published.

LINDSEY HOLLAND grew up in Aughton, on the Lancashire border with Merseyside. She studied at the University of Warwick for several years, gaining an MA in Writing before moving back to her hometown. She teaches poetry on the Creative Writing programme at Edge Hill University, where she is also working towards a Creative Writing PhD. Her poetry and reviews have appeared in various magazines and anthologies including *Tears in the Fence, The New Writer, B O D Y, Ink Sweat & Tears, Sabotage Reviews, Penning Perfumes, Estuary* and *Lung Jazz: Young British Poets for Oxfam.* Her collection, *Particle Soup* (2012), is available from The Knives Forks and Spoons Press.

SARAH JAMES is an award-winning and widely published journalist, fiction writer and poet, currently studying for an MA in Creative Writing (online poetry route) at Manchester Metropolitan University. Her first poetry collection *Into the Yell* (Circaidy Gregory Press, 2010) won third prize in the International Rubery Book Award 2011 and she is now working on her second collection. She also enjoys performance poetry and artistic collaborations. The 37-year-old mother-of-two's many other shape-shifting roles include sky-watcher, chaos-catcher, time-squeezer, quiet-seeker...and she is a compulsive list-maker too! Her website and blog are at: www.sarah-james.co.uk .

EVAN JONES is a Canadian poet who has lived in Manchester since 2005. His most recent book is *Paralogues* (Carcanet 2012).

CLARE KIRWAN is based in Wirral. Her poems have been widely published in magazines including *MsLexia, Orbis, The Interpreter's House* and *The Found Poetry Review* as well as in various anthologies. She has been Liverpool Poetry Slam champion and has been placed in a number of poetry competitions from Big Issue to Feile Filiochta. She founded poetry site Poetry24 — 'where news is the muse' — and also writes fiction.

KEITH LANDER has lived in the North West for most of his life apart from a few years working in Germany. His poems have appeared in *The North, Envoi, Borderlines, Bewilderbliss* and *Turbulence*. A software engineer by trade, he has devoted much time to learning the craft of poetry in the form of an MA from MMU, several Arvon courses, and far too many workshops. He maintains the Dear List started by Linda Chase and was an early member of the Poets & Players advisory group.

MELISSA LEE-HOUGHTON's first collection, *A Body Made of You*, is published by Penned in the Margins. Her work has been published widely in magazines, most recently *Tears in the Fence, Under the Radar* and *The Reader*. She is a contributor to *The Silent History*, a digital novel for iPad and iPhone. She writes reviews for *The Short Review*.

JOHN LINDLEY is a freelance poet and creative writing tutor. An experienced performer, he has read at Ledbury Poetry Festival and at the Buxton and Edinburgh Fringe Festivals. He runs poetry workshops for writers' groups, festivals and in prisons, schools, universities and day care centres, as well as for those with learning difficulties. Widely published, he has been a prizewinner in a number of national competitions. His latest collection is *The Casting Boat* (Headland, 2009). A new collection, *Screen Fever,* is to be published by Pinewood Press in September 2012.

LIZ LOXLEY lives in Flintshire with her civil partner, who is also a poet. Her poems have been anthologised by publishers including Faber, Penguin and Oxford University Press, have appeared in various poetry magazines and have been studied by school students. Liz is now studying for an MA in Creative Writing (Poetry) at Manchester Metropolitan University.

EMMA McCOURTY lives and works in Cheshire. Her first poetry collection, *Everynothing*, was published in 2010 by The Knives Forks and Spoons Press. She has performed her work at guest slots around the North West.

GILL McEVOY has published two pamphlets: *Uncertain Days* (Happenstance Press, 2006) and *A Sampler* (Happenstance Press, 2008). A full collection, *The Plucking Shed*, was published by Cinnamon Press in 2010 and her second collection *Rise* is forthcoming from Cinnamon in 2013. Gill has been awarded a Hawthornden Fellowship for

2012. She runs The Poem Shed, the Golden Pear poetry reading group and, together with friends, Zest! Open floor poetry nights in Chester.

RACHEL McGLADDERY is a poet living in rural Lancashire. She writes about the people, places and politics of the North West. She has had her work published online, in magazines and in anthologies, the latest being *Estuary* to be launched in December 2012. Equally at home on the page or stage, Rachel won the Liverpool Lennon Performance Poetry Prize in 2010.

ANDREW MCMILLAN was born in 1988 and lives in central Manchester; his poetry is collected in three pamphlets including *the moon is a supporting player* (Red Squirrel Press, 2011) and *protest of the physical* (Holdfire Press 2012). A selection of work is also included in the *Salt Book of Younger Poets*.

KIM MOORE won an Eric Gregory Award and the Geoffrey Dearmer Prize in 2011. Her pamphlet *If We Could Speak Like Wolves* was a winner in the Poetry Business 2012 Pamphlet Competition. Her writing placements include Young Writer-in-Residence at the Ledbury 2012 Poetry Festival.

DAVID MORLEY's recently published *Enchantment* (Carcanet) was a *Sunday Telegraph* Book of the Year chosen by Jonathan Bate. *The Invisible Kings* was a PBS Recommendation and *TLS* Book of the Year chosen by Les Murray. *The Gypsy and the Poet* is due from Carcanet in 2013 followed by *New and Selected Poems* in 2014. He writes regularly for *The Guardian* and *Poetry Review*. He wrote *The Cambridge Introduction to Creative Writing* and co-edited *The Cambridge Companion to Creative Writing*. He teaches at Warwick University where he is Professor of Writing. www.davidmorley.org.uk

CATH NICHOLS has worked in the North West all her adult life: in Manchester in mental health, then radio and journalism; in Liverpool for the Dead Good Poets Society. She has a PhD in Creative Writing from Lancaster University and lives near Warrington. Her pamphlets are *Tales of Boy Nancy*, 2005, and *Distance*, 2012, and her full-length collection is *My Glamorous Assistant* (2007). *Do you take sugar?* a radio-poetry play for BBC Radio Lancashire, appeared in 2007 and *The Price of Legs* was produced for the Triliteral Stageplay Festival in 2010. Cath is currently adapting the play into a children's novel.

ANDREW OLDHAM is an award winning writer and poet. His poetry has been heard on BBC Radio Four's *Poetry Please* and been read in *Ambit*, *The London Magazine*, *Interpreter's House*, *North American Review* and *Poetry Salzburg*. Andrew is a past Jerwood-Arvon nominee. His first collection, *Ghost of a Low* Moon was published by Lapwing, Belfast in 2010 to critical acclaim, 'One of the brightest and most memorable British poetic voices of today'. - Vince Gotera, Editor, *North American Review.* He lives in Saddleworth where he curses rain and climbs trees to face north winds. www.andrewoldham.co.uk

DANIELE PANTANO is a Swiss poet, translator, critic, and editor born of Sicilian and German parentage in Langenthal (Canton of Berne). His most recent works include *The Possible Is Monstrous: Selected Poems by Friedrich Dürrenmatt*, *The Oldest Hands in the World*, *Oppressive Light: Selected Poems by Robert Walser* (all from Black Lawrence Press/Dzanc Books, 2010 – 12), as well as *Mass Graves (XIX-XXII)* and *Mass Graves: City of Now* (both from Knives, Forks and Spoons Press, 2011 – 12). His forthcoming books include *Mass Graves: A Confession* and *The Collected Works of Georg Trakl.* For more information, please visit www.danielepantano.ch

STEPH PIKE is a Manchester based performance poet. She has performed extensively across the North West and has been published in several anthologies. She has produced 5 minute word portraits as part of a human photo booth and is the Sheffield Grand Dame of Slam 2011. Her first collection of poetry *Full of the Deep Bits* was published in 2010 by The Knives Forks and Spoons Press. Steph runs a poetry night in Manchester called 'Word Up'.

JANINE PINION is based in Wirral, Merseyside. She moved from Belfast to study at Liverpool College of Art and has exhibited in the North West and Ireland, and had poems published in magazines and anthologies including *Ambit*, *Iota* and *Interpreters House*. Driftwood published her pamphlet in 2003 and she is currently writing a full collection. Janine teaches in higher education and mental health. Her poetry has been described as visual and enticing, based on subjects such as an Irish childhood, missing people and postcards of modern life. She also enjoys maps, walking and windsurfing.

SIAN S. RATHORE is a poet, critic and journalist who writes for *Huffington Post*, *Thought Catalog*, *Alt Lit Gossip* and *Stride*, and whose poetry has appeared in many online and print journals including a forthcoming collection for *3:AM*. She is an editor for Canadian lit-zine *Metazen*, and runs an online journal of art and literature called *Sadcore Dadwave*. Rathore is 23, and living somewhere inbetween.

ELEANOR REES was born in Birkenhead, Merseyside in 1978. Her pamphlet collection *Feeding Fire* received an Eric Gregory Award in 2002 and her first full length collection *Andraste's Hair* (Salt, 2007) was shortlisted for the Forward Prize for Best First Collection and the Glen Dimplex New Writers Awards. Her second collection *Eliza and the Bear* (Salt, 2009) is also a live performance for voice and harp which has toured in the North West. Rees works in the community as a poet, running writing workshops for The Windows Project, as a freelancer and is also studying for an AHRC funded PhD University of Exeter in the theory and practice of the local poet. She often collaborates with other writers, musicians and artists and works to commission. She lives in Liverpool. www.eleanorrees.info

DAVID RILEY lives in Blackpool and is a writer of poetry and plays. He is particularly interested in ekphrasis in poetry and has published several poetic works connected to visual art, working especially with other North West poets and a painter living on the Fylde Coast. He is also interested in the idea of time and how it is handled in poetic works.

MICHAEL SYMMONS ROBERTS was born in 1963 in Preston, Lancashire. His poetry has won the Whitbread Poetry Award, and been shortlisted for the Griffin International Poetry Prize, the Forward Prize, and twice for the T.S. Eliot Prize. He has received major awards from the Arts Council and the Society of Authors. As a librettist he has written BBC Proms choral commissions, song cycles and operas for the Royal Opera House, Scottish Opera, Boston Lyric Opera and Welsh National Opera. *The Sacrifice* won the RPS Award and *Clemency* was nominated for an Olivier Award. He is Professor of Poetry at Manchester Metropolitan University.

JONNY RODGERS is a poet from the North West. He completed an MA in Post-1900 Theories, Literatures and Cultures at Manchester University and his publications include *Puppywolf's Best of Manchester Poets*, *Prole*, *The Delinquent*, and *Ink, Sweat and Tears*.

JANET ROGERSON's pamphlet *A Bad Influence Girl* was published by *The Rialto* in 2012. She is a PhD student at the University of Manchester.

PAULINE ROWE lives in Liverpool with her husband and 6 children. She has two pamphlets, a full collection, *Waiting for the Brown Trout God* (Headland Publications, 2009), a libretto (*Benares*, 2005) and a poetry film (*Nothing Rhymes With Poets* — First Take, 2006). She works as a poet and writer especially in mental health and community settings. She is founder member and co-ordinator of the charity, North End Writers.

ANDREW RUDD lives in Frodsham, in Cheshire, and was Cheshire Poet Laureate in 2006. His poetry collections are *One Cloud Away from the Sky* (2007) and *Nowhere Else but Here* (2012). He has published in *The North*, *The SHOp*, *Smiths Knoll*, *Best of Manchester Poets*, *Scintilla*, *Staple* and *Other Poetry*. He has twice won the Cheshire Prize for Literature, and came second in the Ledbury Competition. His poems have appeared on Radio 4, and he toured with two poetry shows: 'Bunch of Fives' and 'Fourpenny Circus'. He works at MMU with primary teachers, and also teaches on the Creative Writing MA.

DAVID SEDDON was born in Liverpool and now lives in Congleton, Cheshire where he is a counsellor. He has many poems published in various ezines and magazines including *Poetry Scotland*, *Poetry Cornwall*, *Sonnetto Poesia*, *Earth Love*, *Decanto*, *Sarasvati* and *The Tower Journal*. He is also in the Macmillan Cancer Charity Anthology, *Soul Feathers* and the *Robin Hood Verse Versus Austerity* Anthology and has been in *Poems in the Waiting Room*. He is a co-editor of the forthcoming Sonnet Anthology, *The Phoenix Rising From The Ashes*. He is actively pursuing getting his first collection of poems out.

ROBERT SHEPPARD lives in Liverpool and teaches at Edge Hill University, which is not at Edge Hill, Liverpool, but in Ormskirk. He blew in during 1996 and has published a number of books since then, including *Complete Twentieth Century Blues* (Salt, 2008), *Berlin Bursts* (Shearsman, 2011) and *The Given* (Knives, Forks and Spoons, 2010). All three contain texts about Liverpool, none about Ormskirk. Despite this, he is still described as a 'London poet'. He is also a critic and has published books on contemporary poetry and Iain Sinclair.

JOHN SIDDIQUE was born in the North West. He is the author of *Full Blood*, *Recital — An Almanac*, *Poems From A Northern Soul*, *The Prize* and the co-author of the story/memoir *Four Fathers*. His work has featured in many places, including *Granta*, *The Guardian*, *Poetry Review* and

192

BBC RADIO 4. *The Spectator* refers to him as 'A stellar British poet'. *The Times of India* calls him 'Rebellious by nature, pure at heart'. Novelist Bina Shah says he is 'One of the best poets of our generation'. He is the Honorary Creative Writing Fellow at Leicester University.

JACOB SILKSTONE graduated from the Creative Writing MA at Lancaster University with a distinction and has recently worked as a primary school teacher in Bangladesh. He is a poetry editor for *The Missing Slate* and an assistant editor for *Asymptote*. He has previously been published in a number of magazines, both in print and online.

ADRIAN SLATCHER is originally from Staffordshire but moved to the North West aged 18, to study English at Lancaster, and has subsequently settled in Manchester, where he has lived for nearly 20 years. He has written fiction, poetry and music, been published widely, and has two poetry selections available, *Playing Solitaire for Money* (Salt, 2010) and *Extracts from Levona* (Knives, Forks and Spoons, 2010).

V.A. SOLA SMITH was born in 1988, in Lancashire. She took a Contemporary Prose Fiction MA, at Kingston University, graduating with Distinction in 2010.

EDWIN STOCKDALE graduated from Lancaster University in 2007 after studying Creative Writing and Music. Recent magazine publications include the *Brontë Society Gazette*, the *Coffee House*, *Drey (Red Squirrel Press)*, *ink sweat & tears*, the *Interpreter's House*, *In the Red*, *Obsessed with Pipework*, *Open Mouse (Poetry Scotland)*, *Poetry Salzburg Review*, *Poetry Cornwall*, *Poetry Scotland* and *Snakeskin*. Edwin has just completed his postgraduate training at Liverpool Hope University to be a primary school and nursery teacher.

ALICIA STUBBERSFIELD has published three collections of poetry and her fourth, *The Yellow Table*, is forthcoming from Pindrop Press in 2013. She is one of the judges for the prestigious 2012 Aldeburgh Poetry Festival First Collection Prize and also judges the writing entries for The Koestler Awards for Prison Art & Writing in the North. A tutor of courses for The Arvon Foundation, The Taliesin Trust at Ty Newydd and The Poetry School, she is Senior Lecturer in Creative Writing at Liverpool John Moores University.

DAVID TAIT grew up in Lancaster and now lives in Hebden Bridge. He's had poems in *Magma, Poetry Review* and *The Rialto* and his pamphlet *Love's Loose Ends* won the 2011 Poetry Business Pamphlet Competition. He is House Poet at Manchester Royal Exchange for the Carol Ann Duffy & Friends Poetry Series.

ANDREW TAYLOR is a Liverpool poet and co-editor of *erbacce* and erbacce-press. After several pamphlets, his first full collection *Radio Mast Horizon* is published by Shearsman. Poems have recently appeared in *Poetry Wales, The Red Ceilings, Instant Pussy* and *Alligator Stew.* A founder member of the Edge Hill University Poetry and Poetics Research Group, he gained a PhD under the supervision of the poet and critic Robert Sheppard.

SCOTT THURSTON'S books include: *Reverses Heart's Reassembly* (Veer Books, 2011), *Of Being Circular* (The Knives Forks and Spoons Press, 2010), *Internal Rhyme* (Shearsman, 2010), *Momentum* (Shearsman, 2008), and *Hold* (Shearsman, 2006). He edits *The Radiator* (a little magazine of poetics), co-edits *The Journal of British and Irish Innovative Poetry* and co-organises the Manchester-based poetry reading series The Other Room. Scott lectures in English and Creative Writing at the University of Salford and has published widely on innovative poetry, including a recent book of interviews *Talking Poetics* (Shearsman, 2011). He lives in Toxteth, Liverpool 8. See his pages at www.archiveofthenow.com

ANGELA TOPPING is a freelance poet, author and former teacher/lecturer. Her ninth poetry publication is *Paper Patterns* (Lapwing Press). Previous collections were with

Stride (1988 & 1989; a new and selected 1999); bluechrome (2007) and Salt (2010 and 2011). She also had a Rack Press pamphlet (2011) and two chapbooks (Erbacce, including *The Lightfoot Letters*, which accompanied an art/poetry exhibition in 2011). Poems have appeared in magazines including *Poetry Review*, *London Magazine* and *Agenda* and are set for A level. She has edited and co-edited several poetry anthologies, and written critical books. She is also well known for her children's poetry. In October 2013 she will take up a residency at Gladstone's Library, Hawarden.

STEVEN WALING is a widely-published poet, who collections include *Calling Myself On the Phone* (Smith/Doorstep) and *Travelator* (Salt). He has edited books for Crocus, has been a Writer in Prison and mentored the poetry of African writers through the British Council/Lancaster University Crossing Borders scheme. He is a trustee of the Commonword Trust, and has taught creative writing and has performed his poetry in many venues from Edinburgh to Johannesburg.

DAVE WARD's poetry has appeared in over 100 anthologies from Faber, Puffin, Viking and Macmillan and on BBC TV and radio. Publications include *Tracts* (Headland), *Jambo* (Impact), *The Tree of Dreams* (HarperCollins) and *Candy & Jazzz* (OUP). He is co-founder of The Windows Project, co-ordinating writing workshops throughout Merseyside and the North West; and co-editor of *Smoke* magazine.

JT WELSCH was born in St. Louis, completed an MA at Royal Holloway and PhD at the University of Manchester, and is currently lecturer in Creative Writing and English Literature at York St John University. His plays have been staged at the Manchester Library Theatre and Martin Harris Centre for Drama in Manchester, and his poetry has appeared in *Boston Review*, *Stand*, *Manchester Review*, *Blackbox Manifold*, and the chapbooks, *Orchids* (Salt 2010),

Orchestra & Chorus (Holdfire 2012), and *Waterloo* (Like This 2012).

JOY WINKLER's work has been published in various magazines and she has had success in many competitions. She has had three collections of poetry published including the most recent, *On the Edge*. She is a former Cheshire Poet Laureate and has toured with other poets as 'Bunch of Fives' and 'Fourpenny Circus', delivering innovatory poetry performance across the North West. Joy facilitates workshops and projects in the North West area, in particular with groups in Macclesfield, Salford and Rochdale. She was writer in residence in HMP Styal for 7 years and is part of the Writers in Prison Network.

ACKNOWLEDGMENTS

ALISON CHISHOLM: 'On the Brink' from *Iced* (Caleta Publishing, 2012). Copyright © Alison Chisholm.

MARTIN FIGURA: 'AHEM' from *Ahem* (Eggbox Publishing, 2005) and *Boring The Arse Off Young People* (Nasty Little Press, 2010). Also appeared in *The Rialto* (2005). Copyright © Martin Figura.

EVAN JONES: 'Cavafy in Liverpool' from *Paralogues* (Carcanet, 2012). First appeared in the American literary journal *Agni*. Copyright © Evan Jones.

JOHN LINDLEY: 'Ellesmere Port' was included in *The Casting Boat* (Headland, 2009) under the title *Identity*. It also appeared on a DVD entitled *Our Town* (Arts Council North West). Copyright © John Lindley.

GILL McEVOY: 'Blakemere, Cheshire' appeared in *Orbis*. Reprinted by permission of the poet.

KIM MOORE: 'Train Journey, Barrow to Sheffield' from *If We Could Speak Like Wolves* (Smith/Doorstop, 2012). Copyright © Kim Moore.

CATH NICHOLS: 'Miss Lydia Rawlinson takes her tea with sugar' is part of a radio script commissioned by Lancaster Litfest for BBC Radio Lancashire in 2007. Printed here by permission of the poet.

ANDREW OLDHAM: 'The Last Time We Met' appears in *The Anchor* (Glass Head Press, 2012). Copyright © Andrew Oldham. 'Two Thousand Year Stare' is taken from *Ghosts of a Low Moon* by Andrew Oldham, (Lapwing, Belfast, 2010). Copyright © Andrew Oldham.

DANIELE PANTANO: 'Vaudeville' appeared in *Shipwrights* (2011). Reprinted by permission of the poet.

ELEANOR REES: 'Saltwater' from *A Burial of Sight* (The Word Hoard, 2012). Originally a commission by Almanac for 'Radical